HARDY

# MAYOR
# OF
# CASTERBRIDGE

## NOTES

COLES EDITORIAL BOARD

Bound to stay open

**Publisher's Note**

Otabind (Ota-bind). This book has been bound using the patented Otabind process. You can open this book at any page, gently run your finger down the spine, and the pages will lie flat.

## ABOUT COLES NOTES

COLES NOTES have been an indispensible aid to students on five continents since 1948.

COLES NOTES are available for a wide range of individual literary works. Clear, concise explanations and insights are provided along with interesting interpretations and evaluations.

Proper use of COLES NOTES will allow the student to pay greater attention to lectures and spend less time taking notes. This will result in a broader understanding of the work being studied and will free the student for increased participation in discussions.

COLES NOTES are an invaluable aid for review and exam preparation as well as an invitation to explore different interpretive paths.

COLES NOTES are written by experts in their fields. It should be noted that any literary judgement expressed herein is just that – the judgement of one school of thought. Interpretations that diverge from, or totally disagree with any criticism may be equally valid.

COLES NOTES are designed to supplement the text and are not intended as a substitute for reading the text itself. Use of the NOTES will serve not only to clarify the work being studied, but should enhance the readers enjoyment of the topic.

**ISBN 0-7740-3311-8**

© COPYRIGHT 1998 AND PUBLISHED BY
**COLES PUBLISHING COMPANY**
TORONTO - CANADA
PRINTED IN CANADA

Manufactured by Webcom Limited
Cover finish: Webcom's Exclusive **DURACOAT**

# CONTENTS

# Thomas Hardy: Life and Works

Thomas Hardy was born on June 2, 1840, in the village of Higher Bockhampton, about three miles from the town of Dorchester in southwestern England. The impressions of his early youth — the people, the events, the countryside — became part of the subject matter of his "Wessex" novels and stories. The town of Casterbridge itself, for example, is modelled after Dorchester.

Hardy's father was a builder and stonemason and was by no means wealthy. His mother loved reading, and, under her care, young Thomas was given an ample introduction to the classics, folk songs, ballads, and local stories and legends. Music was also a feature of the Hardy household. Thomas' father taught him to play the violin, for he was violinist in the church choir and often played at parties, weddings and festivals. Music was a great love throughout Thomas Hardy's life and often figures in his writing. At least three important scenes in *The Mayor of Casterbridge* involve music.

Hardy did not study at a university. His formal education consisted of a year in a village school at Lower Bockhampton and additional private schooling in Dorchester, during which he learned French and German. When he was 16, his father apprenticed him to a Dorchester architect, John Hicks, where he was taught architectural drawing for the restoration of churches and old houses. This association taught him much of local family histories and folklore. When the day's work was completed, Thomas usually undertook advanced Latin studies and the task of teaching himself Greek.

In 1862, Hardy went to London as a draftsman and worked in the office of A.W. Blomfield, an architect. During this time, he won a number of prizes for essays and began to steep himself in architectural and art studies, classic literature, contemporary poetry and fiction. In 1867, he returned to Dorchester to a better position, as a church restorer with his former master, and began to write more steadily.

From this time on, Hardy wrote poetry and novels, though he dedicated himself chiefly to the novel until 1895. His novels were published, for the most part, in serial form in well-known magazines both in England and America. His major novels are: *Under the Greenwood Tree* (1872), *Far from the Madding Crowd*

1

(1874), *The Return of the Native* (1878), *The Mayor of Caster-bridge* (1886), *The Woodlanders* (1887), *Tess of the D'Urbervilles* (1891) and *Jude the Obscure* (1895). His works were highly acclaimed (the success of *Far from the Madding Crowd* enabled him to give up architecture and to marry), but he also encountered literary hostility. *Jude the Obscure* received such harsh criticism that Hardy gave up the writing of novels entirely.

Hardy retired to his house in Dorchester and there turned to poetry almost exclusively. Before his death he completed more than 800 poems and a long epic drama, *The Dynasts* (1908). His first marriage was not happy, and, in 1914, two years after the death of his first wife, he married a second time. The remaining years of his life were spent in matrimonial devotion and tranquillity.

The last two decades of Hardy's life were increasingly full of honors. With George Meredith's death in 1909, Hardy became undisputed holder of the title of greatest living man of letters and, in 1910, he was awarded the Order of Merit. His house, Max Gate, became a literary shrine, and there he received many visitors from all over the English-speaking world. He continued to publish poetry well into the 1920s, even though he was then over 80. He died at the age of 87 on January 11, 1928.

# The World of Thomas Hardy

The Victorian period has been described as a peaceful, complacent and intellectually stagnant age. Actually, the opposite view is more accurate. The Victorian period was a violent, disturbed and revolutionary age. Let us examine some of the changes that occurred during this time, as background to Hardy's works.

## An Era of Change

The nineteenth century was marked by changes in society, in politics, in religion and in art. Changes in the social structure resulted in shifts in political power. England experienced what modern economists call "take-off" — the emergence from rigid economic and political structures into the dynamic world of modern capitalism. For England, this change had begun in the eighteenth century and, by Hardy's time, the rapidity of the change was violent, almost chaotic. The effects of this change are well-known: England was transformed from a rural and agricultural nation, with a population distributed fairly uniformly throughout the country, into an industrial and urban nation, with a population tending to gather, for better or worse, in the large cities. Hardy refers to these changes in *The Mayor of Casterbridge.*

## Population Growth

Britain, locked as it is on two small islands, was the first modern country to be seriously concerned with a population explosion. That concern may be seen as early as Adam Smith's *Wealth of Nations* (1776) and Thomas Malthus' *Essay on the Principle of Population* (1798), but the concern intensified throughout a century during which Britain's population quadrupled.

## Urbanization

The problem of this population explosion, serious in itself, was aggravated by the collection of these masses of people in the new urban centers resulting from introduction of the factory system during the Industrial Revolution. In the eighteenth century, English textile industry was based on the work done in thousands of cottages in rural areas. While the farmer tended his small garden plot, family income might be supplemented by weaving done by his wife and daughters on small looms. With the invention of the power loom and related equipment, machinery became too unwieldy and too expensive for the individual farmer. The only people who could afford to operate and maintain the huge machines were the "captains of industry," the new "middle class," who could set up their equipment in central locations. The farmer, unable to support himself without the additional income of his wife, was driven off the farm and into the city. Birmingham, Manchester, London, Liverpool and many other large cities became huge dumping spots for millions of agricultural workers driven from the land.

## Politics

The changes in society naturally resulted in changes in political structure. It has been said that Queen Victoria's reign proved that England could do without a monarch. Certainly, the traditional institutions of king and royalty were being eroded. A new middle class of industrialists and merchants arose. Shifts in population raised questions of reapportionment and demands for extension of voting rights to the middle class, later to the lower classes and, finally, to women. In politics, as in society, change became a way of life, distasteful to many, but apparently unavoidable.

## Religion

Such large external changes were parallelled by changes in ways of thinking and in attitudes. Most critical here was the assault on traditional religion, either as represented in fundamental beliefs or through formal rituals and organizations. One may argue that the "romantic revolution" of the first part of the century had been an attempt to retain a "religious" or "illusioned" view of life. The progress of the rest of the century was in the direction of "dis-illusionment," or a casting-off — often regretfully — of religious interpretations of man and his place in the universe.

### A New View of the Bible

Some Christians were concerned with the so-called "higher criticism" imported from Germany and France. This teaching called into question the traditional belief that the Bible was the word of God. Ernest Renan in France and David F. Strauss in

Germany wrote influential books that attempted to "demythologize" the Bible by presenting a "historical Jesus." Matthew Arnold, among others in England, urged that the modern Christian rid himself of the superstitions and myths that had accumulated around the spirit of Christianity. During the Victorian period, then, men were examining, testing and criticizing the Bible. For many, this testing had shattering effects of their personal faith.

## A New View of Nature

The other traditional proof of God's goodness was nature: "the heavens declare the glory of God." Unfortunately, this other refuge of belief was being destroyed by the advance of science. Each advance in biology and geology seemed to show more clearly that nature was, in Tennyson's words, "red in tooth and claw." The laws of nature, far from being beneficent to man or appearing controlled by a rational deity, seemed to work capriciously, even malevolently. Not only did individuals disappear, struck down by chance or accident, without any apparent purpose behind their lives, but whole species appeared in the vast span of time, lived briefly (in terms of millions of years) and were ruthlessly wiped out, again for no apparent reason.

## Darwinism

The key figure here, of course, was Charles Darwin, whose *The Origin of Species* (1859) must be recognized as one of the turning points in Western intellectual history. Actually, Darwin's work was a culmination of the work of many others, "evolutionists" extending back to the eighteenth century. Although many of Darwin's conclusions have proved inadequate, *The Origin of Species* is important because it was the first book to support the evolutionary hypothesis with a mass of scientific data, evidence that Darwin had patiently accumulated for years. All other arguments — such as the sensational debates over man's descent from the monkey, or the existence of a "missing link" — are insignificant in comparison to the evidence that Darwin presented. It was difficult to deny that species were mutable and that they seemed to change largely through accident in order to accommodate themselves to their environment. Furthermore, it seemed to many that God did not enter into this rather disorderly

5

state of affairs. In the 1880s, Nietzsche was to summarize the bleak situation with his agonized cry, "God is dead."

Hardy was affected by this intellectual doubt, and yet he had a strong sense of a power beyond human control or understanding. He frequently referred to this power as "fate" or "destiny" in his novels. The philosophy expressed in Hardy's novels is usually expressed by the characters themselves. He integrates intellectual ideas into his novels by linking ideas to his characters and to their situations.

Hardy was a popular Victorian novelist. He did not evade the issues raised by economic, social and religious changes. Refusing to ignore the darker sides of human nature, he was strongly criticized for his attempt to be honest in treating sexual matters and in recognizing the sorrow and pain of human life. Hardy refused to please his readers with sentimental, happy stories. He insisted on the truth of what he wrote, and his emphasis on sorrow was an attempt to be realistic about human experience. Hardy was a Victorian, but his novels offer studies of human nature not limited by the historical circumstances of their author.

## Hardy's Wessex

In his novels, Hardy described the people and countryside of the southwest of England. The region was called Wessex when it was a Saxon kingdom, and Hardy adopted the name for his fictional country.

He drew on his own experience of the region and studied the dialect and customs of the country people. His novels often take place in the recent past: *The Mayor of Casterbridge* begins in the late 1820s, has its main action in the late 1860s and was written in the 1880s. By writing about the past, Hardy was able to record lost customs, such as the skimmity ride, a rowdy procession intended to mock a man whose wife was shrewish or unfaithful. He also was able to describe the transition from traditional to modern methods in farming.

Hardy chose to limit the settings of his novels to the region in which he lived so that his descriptions and characters would be realistic. However, he did not simply record his impressions and observations. He was an artist, not a sociologist, and he created a fictional world. His novels describe the complexities of human nature and pose questions about human life. The Wessex setting makes his novels more vivid and serves as a background for Hardy's character studies.

# Introduction to *The Mayor of Casterbridge*

*The Mayor of Casterbridge* was published in weekly instalments in a magazine called *The Graphic*, in 1886. It appeared as a book in two volumes in May of the same year. Although Hardy was influenced by the desire to have "some striking episode" in each instalment, he actually completed the novel before serial publication began. Thus, he was able to design the book so as to unify the striking episodes.

The main source of this unity is the emphasis on a single main character, Michael Henchard. The novel's subtitle, "A Story of a Man of Character," introduces this unity. The novel's complete title is *The Life and Death of the Mayor of Casterbridge*. In this portrait of one man, Hardy uses the pattern of tragedy. This man's rise and fall are the result of his own character and, to a lesser extent, of chance, or fate.

Every page of Hardy's Wessex novels displays the influence of Hardy's upbringing, regional background and architectural studies. His characters are at all times real, for they are based on people he had grown up with, people he had heard about in legends and ballads, and people whose tragic histories he had unearthed during his early architectural apprenticeship. There are also long, well-wrought passages describing the countryside, the buildings, the roads, the commerce and the amusements that make up the environment of Casterbridge. Hardy's naturalness in handling this particular environment, which he calls Wessex, infuses the work with a life and reality all its own.

Hardy's philosophy dramatizes the human condition as a struggle between man and man, and between man and his fate. Fate is all-powerful, and, in its blindness, pays no heed to human suffering. This malevolence of fate certainly seems to be demonstrated in *The Mayor of Casterbridge*. Yet the victim of fate, Henchard, is also the "man of character" referred to in the subtitle. The suffering he endures is the result of his actions. Hardy quotes the saying, "Character is Fate," to suggest the real nature of fate. The novel ends on a note of hope because of Henchard's strength of will and his determination to undergo suffering and deprivation to atone for his sins. It is this element that makes the book a unique outgrowth of Hardy's philosophy.

It was natural that the events of his age should have created in Hardy a deep pessimism, but it was also natural that his creative vision as an artist revealed, in *The Mayor of Casterbridge*, a solution to the dilemma: man will overcome because he has the nobility and strength to endure.

# Characters in the Novel

**Michael Henchard:** the mayor of Casterbridge. He begins his career as a hay trusser, rises to the status of gentleman-merchant, then mayor.

**Susan Henchard (Newson):** Michael's wife. She is sold to Newson, the sailor. She is trusting, naïve and somewhat passive, although she does show some strength of will when she is pushed too far.

**Richard Newson:** a good-natured, easygoing sailor who "purchases" Susan. He proves to be a kind companion to her and a loving father to their daughter.

**Elizabeth-Jane Newson:** a quiet and unassuming, but intelligent girl. Her affectionate nature is apparent in her treatment of her mother, Susan, and of Henchard.

**Donald Farfrae:** the young Scotsman who stops in Casterbridge on his way to America and is persuaded by Henchard to stay. He first marries Lucetta Templeman, then Elizabeth-Jane.

**Lucetta Templeman (Le Sueur):** a Frenchwoman whose indiscretion with Henchard caused a scandal in her native town on the island of Jersey. She comes to Casterbridge to marry Henchard, but marries Farfrae instead.

**Joshua Jopp:** Henchard's spiteful, one-time manager. He seeks revenge on Farfrae for taking his job as manager, and is instrumental in arranging the skimmity ride.

**Abel Whittle:** a slow-witted worker who enrages Henchard and unintentionally causes the beginning of the rift between Henchard and Farfrae. He takes care of Henchard at his death, in gratitude for Henchard's kindness to his mother.

**Mrs. Goodenough:** the woman who sells furmity and who reveals Henchard's shameful past to the town.

**Solomon Longways:** one of the townspeople, who is impressed with Farfrae. He writes a letter to Farfrae, luring him away on the night of the skimmity ride.

# Plot Summary

In a fit of drunken irritation, Michael Henchard, a young, unemployed hay trusser, sells his wife, Susan, and his infant daughter to a sailor during a fair in the village of Weydon-Priors. About 18 years later, Susan and her daughter, Elizabeth-Jane, return to seek him out but are told by the "furmity woman," the old hag whose concoction had made Henchard drunk at the fair, that he has moved to the distant town of Casterbridge. The sailor has been reported lost at sea.

Susan and Elizabeth-Jane, the latter innocent of the shameful sale 18 years before, reach Casterbridge, where they discover that Henchard has become the mayor and one of the wealthiest businessmen in the area. Henchard, out of a sense of guilt, courts Susan in a respectable manner and soon after he remarries her, hoping that one day he will be able to acknowledge Elizabeth-Jane as his daughter.

Concurrently with Susan's return, Henchard hires Donald Farfrae, a young Scotsman, as his business manager. After a short while, Susan dies, and Henchard learns that his own daughter had died many years earlier and that Elizabeth-Jane is really the illegitimate daughter of Newson, the sailor, Susan's second husband.

Lucetta Templeman, a young woman from Jersey with whom Henchard has had a romantic involvement, comes to Casterbridge intending to marry Henchard. She meets Farfrae, however, and the two are attracted. Henchard, disturbed by Farfrae's prestige in the town, has dismissed him, and Farfrae sets up a rival business. Shortly after, Farfrae and Lucetta are married.

Henchard's fortunes continue their decline while Farfrae's advance. When Henchard's successor as mayor dies suddenly, Farfrae becomes mayor. Henchard's ruin is almost completed when the "furmity woman" is arrested as a vagrant in Casterbridge and reveals the transaction two decades earlier when Henchard sold his wife. Then, by a combination of bad luck and mismanagement, Henchard goes bankrupt and is forced to make his living as Farfrae's employee.

Lucetta, now at the height of her fortunes, has staked everything on keeping her past relationship with Henchard a secret. Her old love letters to him, however, find their way into the hands of Henchard's vengeful ex-employee, Jopp, who reveals them to the worst element in the town. They organize a "skimmity ride," in which Henchard and Lucetta are paraded in effigy through the streets. The shock of the scandal kills Lucetta.

Now an almost broken man, Henchard moves to the poorest quarters, where his life is made tolerable only by Elizabeth-Jane's kindness and concern. Even his comfort in her affection is threatened, however, when Newson, the sailor, returns in search of his daughter. Henchard's lie to Newson that Elizabeth-Jane has died is eventually discovered, and Elizabeth-Jane, his last source of comfort, turns against him.

Farfrae, after a period as a widower, renews his interest in Elizabeth-Jane. They are married, and Henchard, when he comes to deliver a wedding gift, finds Newson enjoying his position as the bride's father. Heartbroken at Elizabeth-Jane's rejection of him, Henchard leaves and, shortly afterward, dies in an abandoned hut, attended only by the humblest and simplest of his former workmen. The novel closes when Farfrae and Elizabeth-Jane find the place where he has died and read his terrible will of complete renunciation.

# Chapter by Chapter Summaries and Commentaries

## CHAPTER 1

**Summary**

The story opens early one evening in late summer during the 1820s. Michael Henchard, his wife, Susan, and their baby daughter are travelling toward Weydon-Priors, in Upper Wessex, where a fair is being held. Henchard, a hay trusser, is seeking work. They walk without speaking and meet a man who tells them that they will find no work in the district.

They reach the fair and find only the odds and ends that remain after a day's business is done. Michael is about to enter the liquor booth, but Susan persuades him to take her into the tent where furmity, a dish that she likes, is sold. When they order it, the furmity woman laces Michael's with rum. After he has had four servings, he begins to complain to his fellow guests that his life and prospects have been ruined by his early marriage.

Overhearing an auctioneer selling off the remains of his stock, Michael Henchard offers his wife to anyone who will buy her. Although no one responds, he repeats his offer more than once. Susan protests, and reminds him that he has talked foolishly like this before. When he insists, she says that she wishes someone would buy her. A sailor who has entered the tent agrees to pay five guineas for Susan, if she is willing. Henchard persists, and Susan leaves with the sailor, crying and flinging her wedding ring at her husband.

After the spectators have drifted away, disturbed by what has happened, Henchard falls asleep.

**Commentary**

The drabness of the natural setting as Henchard and Susan approach the town harmonizes with their mood. The indifference and "stale familiarity" of their relationship makes the selling of Susan plausible. Henchard's disappointment at not finding work and the effects of the rum demoralize him so completely that he can go through with the transaction.

The shock of the wife auction compels our attention at the beginning of the novel. Hardy uses the incident to focus on Henchard's impulsiveness, his self-pity and his ambition. The rum heightens Henchard's sense of the injustice of his poverty and his inability to find work to support his family. At the same time, it blunts his sense of the importance of the marriage bond, which he mocks by selling his wife.

Susan is passive and endures her husband's proposals without looking up, "as if she maintained her position by a supreme effort of will." When a sailor agrees to pay five guineas for her, she says to her husband: "It is a joke no longer." She goes with Newson, the sailor, when Henchard refuses to retract his offer. Like her husband, she has a strong sense of justice. Since Henchard rejects his responsibility for her and for their child, she rejects him and accepts Newson's offer of protection. She weeps and throws her wedding ring in anger, but she has the courage to leave.

**fustian:** coarse cotton.
**phlegmatically:** apathetically, indifferently.
**hurdle:** a temporary animal pen.
**thimble-riggers:** conjurers, magicians.
**mincing:** with affected delicacy.
**penuriousness:** poverty.
**'vation:** salvation.
**be-right:** by right, truly.
**rheumy:** sniffling.
**keacorn:** (dialect) throat.

QUESTION: How do you account for the fact that an incident as apparently improbable and melodramatic as the sale of a wife seems believable and holds our attention?

# CHAPTER 2

## Summary
Upon awakening the next morning, Henchard finds Susan's wedding ring on the floor and the sailor's money in his pocket. He now understands that the preceding night's events are not a dream and, "in silent thought," walks away from the village into the country.

He is angry with Susan, but realizes that Susan's simplicity and trusting nature will make her accept what has happened. He recalls her threat to take him at his word.

He decides to search for his wife and child and, when he finds them, to try to live with his shame. First he goes to a church and swears an oath before the altar that he will not touch strong drink "for the space of twenty-one years — a year for every year that I have lived." He begins his search, but no one has any recollection of having seen Susan and the child. His search lasts for months until he learns at a seaport that "persons answering somewhat to his description had emigrated a little time before." He abandons his search and journeys to the town of Casterbridge in a distant part of Wessex.

## Commentary

Henchard's pride and determination are shown in this chapter. He is willing to search for his wife and live with the shame he has brought upon himself, but his pride will not let him reveal to strangers what he has done. He feels relief that he did not state his name during the transaction.

His vow to stop drinking shows his sense of the wrong he has done and his desire to do penance. The strength to impose a penalty on himself and the desire to protect his name are important aspects of Henchard's character. He is also superstitious, as his going to the church to swear the oath shows.

Together, the first two chapters form a prologue to the main action of the novel. They introduce the main characters and describe the event from which the rest of the story develops.

**felloe:** outside rim.
**the Seven Sleepers:** a story in the Koran of seven men who sleep for hundreds of years in a cave.
**fetichistic:** attributing magical power to inanimate objects.
**sacrarium:** the place before the altar.
**strook:** struck.

QUESTION: How is the action of the rest of the novel prepared for in the first two chapters?

## CHAPTER 3

### Summary

The beginning of this chapter parallels the beginning of the novel, as Susan and Elizabeth-Jane walk to the Weydon-Priors fair almost 20 years after Susan walked to the town with Michael Henchard. The two women are in mourning for Richard Newson, the sailor whose name Susan has taken, for he has been lost at sea. They come looking for information about Henchard, in the hope that he may help them. Susan has told Elizabeth-Jane only that Henchard is a relation by marriage.

The furmity woman no longer has a tent, but Susan finds her and asks if she remembers a wife being sold at the fair many years ago. The woman tells her that the man responsible returned about a year after the event and asked her to tell anyone inquiring for him that he was living in Casterbridge.

Susan decides to journey to Casterbridge to find Henchard.

## Commentary

The parallel between the first scene in the novel and the beginning of this chapter emphasizes the difference between the relationship between Susan and her daughter, as they affectionately hold hands, and Susan and her husband, who walked without touching or speaking to each other.

Hardy describes the effects of the passage of time in terms of physical changes, as well as describing the continuity that is unaffected by time. Susan seeks her husband because her bond to the sailor is broken by his death.

Elizabeth-Jane's affection for Newson, her dead father, is evident. Susan's eagerness to find Henchard is the result of need and of affection.

**withy basket:** a basket made of woven willow twigs.
*soi-disant:* calling oneself, so-called.

QUESTION: What do we learn of Susan's character in this chapter?

## CHAPTER 4

### Summary

A flashback reveals that Susan has not told her daughter about the past. She emigrated with Newson to Canada soon after parting from Henchard, and accepted the sailor as her legal husband until a friend to whom she told her story questioned the legal status of the sale. Susan confided her distress to Newson.

When news came that Newson was lost at sea, she set out to find Henchard.

She is anxious to save Elizabeth-Jane from poverty, and can see no other solution to the problem of their condition than the hope that Henchard will be in a position to help them.

When they reach Casterbridge, they hear Henchard's name mentioned. They also hear the townspeople complaining about the poor bread they must eat because the bakers can only buy wheat that has sprouted.

## Commentary

Susan's naïve understanding of her second marriage is an indication of her trusting nature. Her desire to save Elizabeth-Jane from poverty shows love for her daughter and her knowledge of the effects of "that strait-waistcoat of poverty." She recognizes her daughter's intelligence and understands Elizabeth-Jane's desire for knowledge, "to see, to hear, and to understand."

The detailed description of Casterbridge adds realism to the setting. The townspeople's remarks give a context for the introduction of Henchard himself in the next chapter. The mention of Henchard's name increases the suspense of the situation.

**liege subjects of Labour:** laborers as virtually slaves to their work.
**carking:** disturbing, vexing.
**coomb:** the hollow between two hills.
**burgh and champaign:** town and country.
**brick-nogging:** brick work used in filling spaces between boards or beams.
**seed-lips:** seed drills.
**embrocation:** remedies used for bruises.
**pattens:** shoe soles fastened on iron rings to keep the wearer above mud or puddles.
**swipes:** weak beer.
**growed wheat:** wheat that is underdeveloped and sprouts in storage.
**plim:** blown up, swollen.

QUESTION: How has Hardy told the story of Susan's life with Newson to arouse our interest in Elizabeth-Jane and to extend our understanding of Susan's character?

# CHAPTER 5

**Summary**

The mayor is presiding at a great public dinner at the King's Arms when Susan and Elizabeth-Jane arrive in Casterbridge. The windows of the inn are uncovered, so that the townspeople can see the proceedings. Susan is agitated at the prospect of meeting her husband and sends Elizabeth-Jane to inquire among the people outside the inn about Mr. Henchard. Elizabeth-Jane discovers that Henchard is the mayor, and the two women watch him through the windows.

At 40, Henchard is a dynamic, commanding figure. Elizabeth-Jane is surprised by her mother's reaction to the sight of their relative: Susan says, "He overpowers me! I don't wish to see him any more." The change in her husband is so great that Susan is frightened. Although she has resolved to return to him, she is not certain that he will welcome her.

She is encouraged by the fact that he drinks only water. She learns that he has sworn an oath not to touch alcohol for 21 years, and that the period of the oath will expire in two years. She also discovers that Henchard is "a lonely widow man."

Before Susan and Elizabeth-Jane leave, the townspeople protest to Henchard about bad bread made from corn he supplied. He replies that he can do nothing about what has happened, but that he has advertised for a manager to avoid such problems in the future.

**Commentary**

Henchard has become a wealthy and respected citizen. His reaction to the protests about the bad bread shows that he is able to control his temper. His keeping of the oath made after selling his wife is proof of his strength and determination.

Susan is understandably hesitant to make herself known to Henchard. She is poor and her husband is "a pillar of the town." Elizabeth-Jane is ignorant of the true relationship between her mother and Henchard. Thus, she cannot understand why Susan is so afraid of him.

The question of how Henchard will react to Susan's return is a source of suspense.

**fall:** veil

**'a:** he.

**rummers:** a tall stemless drinking glass.

**corn:** (English) grain in general, especially wheat.

**shaken a little to-year:** disturbed or bothered this year.

**cussed:** cursed.

**list:** strip or streak.

QUESTION: Why are we convinced that Henchard, last seen as a drunken unemployed workman, should be the dominant man in a prosperous town?

# CHAPTER 6

## Summary

A stranger, "a young man of remarkably pleasing aspect," hears Henchard dismiss the subject of the sprouted wheat. He writes a note to the mayor, then asks for a respectable, less expensive inn and is directed to the Three Mariners.

Henchard reads the note with interest. He leaves the dinner and follows the stranger to the Three Mariners, where Susan and Elizabeth-Jane have also gone.

## Commentary

The main characters of the story are brought together in one place by chance. Susan has sought Henchard, but the stranger, Farfrae, encounters him accidentally.

Hardy's description of the Three Mariners is detailed. His vivid picture of the inn provides a realistic setting for the characters' encounters.

**mullioned:** glass panes divided into sections by wood or metal bars.

**yard of clay:** long clay pipe.

**ruddy polls:** shiny, bald heads.

**settle:** a long bench with a high back and ends.

QUESTION: What function does the Three Mariners Inn serve in the story apart from providing local color?

# CHAPTER 7

## Summary

Susan is worried that the room they have taken at the Three Mariners is too expensive for them. To ease her mind, Elizabeth-Jane goes downstairs and offers to pay for part of their bill by helping with the serving. She is sent to take a supper tray to the stranger, who is a Scotsman, and whose room adjoins her own.

When the landlady notices how tired Elizabeth-Jane looks, she sends her upstairs to eat with her mother. As the two women eat, they overhear a conversation in the next room between Henchard and the Scotsman, Donald Farfrae.

Farfrae's note had described a chemical process for curing bad wheat, and Henchard offers to pay a good price for the formula. Farfrae says he will explain the method for nothing, because he is on his way to America and has no need of the knowledge.

As they talk, Henchard is greatly taken with the young man and offers him the position of manager. In fact, when Farfrae's note came to him, he had assumed that it was from the man who had applied for the job, Joshua Jopp.

Farfrae refuses Henchard's offer, and the two men part.

Susan hears again about Henchard's 21-year oath of abstinence.

## Commentary

Henchard's response to Farfrae shows that he is a lonely man and that he is impulsive. He is also constantly aware of his guilt in the selling of his wife, as his oath of abstinence shows.

Susan is encouraged by her husband's warmth toward the young man, and Elizabeth-Jane is interested in the Scotsman.

**quag:** abbreviation for quagmire, a bog.

QUESTION: What is the importance of Henchard's forgetting the name of the man who had applied for the job as manager, and his offering the position to someone else?

# CHAPTER 8

## Summary

Leaving Susan, whose face is "strangely bright since

Henchard's avowal of shame for a past action," Elizabeth-Jane watches Farfrae among the guests downstairs. She is too shy to serve on the busy ground floor, but she is attracted to Farfrae and watches him from a corner.

Farfrae sings an emotional song about Scotland, and the guests are moved by his music and his feelings for his country. He sings more songs and captivates the company. When he retires to bed, everyone regrets that he is bound for America instead of settling in Casterbridge.

Elizabeth-Jane, sent to turn down Farfrae's bed, meets him on the stairs as she comes down. He hums a song as they pass.

Susan worries that Elizabeth-Jane shouldn't have worked in the inn, since Henchard's position is so high in the town. Elizabeth-Jane answers that Farfrae is "so respectable and educated" that serving him is a privilege. The chapter ends with a glimpse of Henchard, as he pauses outside the inn in regret at Farfrae's decision to emigrate.

## Commentary

Farfrae's ability to express emotion in his songs surprises the townspeople. His remarks show that he is honest and trusting.

Elizabeth-Jane's interest in Farfrae is a response to his charm and to his educated conversation. She is shy in the presence of the townspeople but is willing to serve the guests, in spite of her shyness, to soothe her mother's worries about money.

The people of Casterbridge speak sometimes in dialect. Their conversation has an undertone of ill humor, although they are openly delighted with Farfrae and his singing.

**danged:** damned.
**lammigers:** lame people.
**ballet:** ballad.
**bruckle:** not trustworthy, unreliable.
**Botany Bay:** a penal colony in Australia.
**chiney:** china.
**chine:** ridge or strip of wood.
**gaberlunzie:** wandering beggar.
**Arthur's Seat:** a hill in Edinburgh.

QUESTION: How does Farfrae's immediate popularity with the townspeople function later in the story?

# CHAPTER 9

## Summary

The next morning, Henchard meets Farfrae outside the inn. Elizabeth-Jane watches the two men walk out of the town together.

Susan is encouraged by her observations of Henchard. She decides to send Elizabeth-Jane to him with a note.

It is market day, and Hardy describes the town's appearance and activities at length. When Elizabeth-Jane reaches Henchard's house, she is surprised to see Farfrae at work in the office. Henchard has been able to persuade the young man to stay as his manager.

## Commentary

The chapter is structured so that Elizabeth-Jane's leisurely walk to Henchard's house takes place while Henchard is persuading Farfrae to stay. The conversation between the two men is presented at the end of the chapter as a flashback.

The description of Casterbridge and the bustling market provides a background for other scenes later in the novel.

Farfrae's absorption in his work allows Elizabeth-Jane to observe him again. He is dedicated to his new job and doesn't recognize her.

*chassez-déchassez:* dancing from right to left.
**Terpsichorean:** from Terpsichore, the Greek muse of dancing.
**staddles:** a platform for stacking hay.
**Cranstoun's Goblin Page:** an elf in Scott's "The Lay of the Last Minstrel."

QUESTION: Why does Farfrae decide to work for Henchard?

# CHAPTER 10

## Summary

While Elizabeth-Jane is waiting to see Henchard, Joshua Jopp, who had applied to become manager, arrives for his interview. Henchard is abrupt with him and announces that the new manager is already at work. Jopp is disappointed and angry.

Henchard treats Elizabeth-Jane kindly. He is moved by her

message that a relative of his, a sailor's widow, is in Casterbridge. He sends a note to Susan, after talking to Elizabeth-Jane about her father's death and asking her about their circumstances. The note is a request that Susan meet him at the Ring, the ruins of a Roman amphitheater just outside the town. He encloses five guineas in the note, to help with her expenses.

## Commentary

Henchard's gesture in enclosing five guineas in his note is a deliberate reminder of his action in selling Susan. By returning the exact amount of the purchase price, he acknowledges his action and shows his desire to make amends to her.

The choice of the ruined amphitheater as the place for their meeting shows Henchard's desire for secrecy until he knows what Susan wants. His inquiry about her financial situation shows his awareness of the needs of others.

Jopp's anger and disappointment make him a potential enemy for both Henchard and Farfrae.

**Bethesda:** the miraculous pool of healing in the Bible.
*rouge-et-noir:* red and black, swarthiness.
**'Josephus':** a Jewish historian, his book.
**'Whole Duty of Man':** a book of devotions.

QUESTION: What clues about future developments does Henchard's note give?

# CHAPTER 11

## Summary

Susan and Henchard meet after dark in the Ring, chosen because of its seclusion. His first words to his wife, "I don't drink ... I haven't since that night," expresses his regret for his action. Susan explains that she assumed her contract with Newson to be binding, and that she returned to look for Henchard only after Newson's death.

Both wish to keep Elizabeth-Jane ignorant of the past. Henchard advises Susan to remain in Casterbridge and to rent a house. He will come to court her, and, in time, they will marry. Elizabeth-Jane will then be his stepdaughter, and the family will be reunited.

Henchard assures Susan that she must look to him for money. She is pleased at the idea of remarrying. When Henchard asks if she can forgive him for the past, her answer is too low to be heard. He asks her to wait and to judge him by the future rather than the past.

## Commentary

Hardy describes the Roman amphitheater carefully to make us feel that the gloom of the place is physical and historical. He uses the Ring as the scene of another encounter later in the novel. Despite the setting, the meeting between Susan and her husband is not melancholy. Henchard has repented and wants to make amends. His plan for their remarriage seems to assure future comfort for Susan and Elizabeth-Jane. Thus, there is a contrast between the gloom of the setting and the hopefulness of the reunion that takes place.

**the Ring:** the Mamebury Rings, just outside Dorchester.
**fibula:** ancient clasp or buckle.
**withered bents:** wiry, half-dead grass.
**Hadrian:** a Roman emperor who visited England.
**Jotuns:** giants in Norse mythology.
**Aeolian modulations:** pleasant, almost musical, sounds; from Aeolus, the Latin god of the wind.

QUESTION: Why does Hardy emphasize the gloomy, unhappy associations of the Ring?

# CHAPTER 12

## Summary

Henchard returns home, finds Farfrae still working over the books and invites him to dinner. After eating, the two men talk. Henchard remarks that he would like to consult his new business partner on a family matter, and Farfrae consents. Henchard confesses his past, and Farfrae agrees that Henchard must make amends for his actions.

The problem is, as Henchard tells his friend, that he has offered to marry a young woman who nursed him while he was sick during a visit to the island of Jersey because her indiscretion in devoting herself to him caused a scandal. Henchard offered to marry her, to save her name, if she were willing to take the chance that his legal wife, Susan, might return. Since Susan has returned, Henchard feels bound to honor his responsibility to her.

Farfrae agrees and helps Henchard by drafting a letter of explanation to the woman in Jersey. Henchard sends this letter and, knowing the woman's financial situation, includes a large sum of money. When he has mailed the letter, he feels free to concentrate on Susan.

Henchard also consults Farfrae about what Elizabeth-Jane should be told of the past. Farfrae suggests revealing everything, but Henchard disagrees. Like Susan, he is hesitant. He resolves to keep his real relationship to Susan a secret from Elizabeth-Jane.

## Commentary

Henchard has known Farfrae only one day, yet he confides the secrets of his past to him. He says that he is a lonely man, and his confidence in his new friend shows that he is also trusting. He is genuinely fond of the Scotsman.

The introduction of the young woman in Jersey suggests a complication in the plan that Henchard proposed to Susan. In spite of the letter of explanation, the possibility of trouble has been suggested. This foreshadowing of difficulty is connected to the gloomy darkness of the scene at the Ring where Henchard and Susan met.

**Jersey:** a British island in the English Channel.
**espaliers:** trellises.
**sequestered:** taken over to settle claims.
**mun:** (dialect) must.

QUESTION: What are the implications of Henchard's confession of his offer to the Jersey woman?

## CHAPTER 13

### Summary

Once Susan and Elizabeth-Jane are settled in a cottage with a servant, Henchard comes to tea. Elizabeth-Jane suspects nothing of the past. After a reasonable period of time, Susan and Henchard decide to marry.

Susan worries that she is causing trouble, but Henchard is

determined to reunite their family and restore her to her rightful place. He is determined to marry her, even though the towns-people think that he is marrying below his position.

The wedding takes place quietly, on a drizzly November day. The local people gather, but they are not impressed by Susan and have nicknamed her "The Ghost" because of her paleness. Christopher Coney, one of the onlookers, says "Daze me if ever I see a man wait so long before to take so little!" His reaction is typical.

## Commentary

The plan is a success, and Henchard marries Susan. Their courtship and wedding are not joyful or exciting events. Susan is distressed at the deception involved but is not willing to explain the past to her daughter.

The reactions of the townspeople to Henchard's sudden fancy for the quiet widow contribute to the feeling of uneasiness. Although Henchard's plan succeeds, it seems threatened by possible difficulties.

Susan's nickname, "The Ghost," is appropriate because she belongs to the past that Henchard had thought dead.

**tumuli:** mounds.
**'en:** him.
**cow-barton:** cow yard.
**"She'll wish her cake dough . . .":** she'll wish she'd married someone with less status (bread as opposed to cake).
**twanking:** whining, complaining.

QUESTION: What significance does the gossip of the townspeople after the wedding have, in view of future events?

# CHAPTER 14

## Summary

Susan is happy when she is settled in Henchard's big house. Although he can give her no deep affection, Henchard is careful to please her in everything.

Elizabeth-Jane enjoys their new position. She feels the peace of security, and her beauty grows. She remains a thoughtful girl, apprehensive in the midst of prosperity, fearing that something dreadful will happen now that everything seems fine. To safeguard against catastrophe, Elizabeth-Jane continues to wear unassuming clothes.

One morning, Henchard carelessly remarks to Susan on the lightness of Elizabeth-Jane's hair, saying that it had been darker when she was a baby. The two manage to pass the remark off without Elizabeth-Jane's noticing it, but they are uneasy at the slip.

Henchard would like Elizabeth-Jane to use his name, but, inexplicably, Susan is opposed to the change. He lets the subject drop, and Elizabeth-Jane keeps her surname of Newson.

Farfrae's careful bookkeeping has brought order to Henchard's business affairs. Elizabeth-Jane's room overlooks the granary yards, and she often sees Farfrae and her stepfather in conversation. She notices that Farfrae often looks closely at Susan, and she wonders if perhaps her mother and Henchard were lovers long ago.

One day, Elizabeth-Jane receives a note asking her to go to the Durnover granary. When she arrives, no one is there. Soon Farfrae arrives with a similar note. The two wonder who could have summoned them, and decide to say nothing about what has happened. Before they leave the granary, Farfrae helps Elizabeth-Jane clean the chaff from her clothes by blowing it off. The meeting brings Elizabeth-Jane and Farfrae together alone for the first time.

## Commentary

Susan's reluctance about the proposal to change Elizabeth-Jane's name suggests that there is something about the girl's parentage that we do not know. Henchard's affection for his stepdaughter and for Farfrae grows, and the meeting of the two in the granary suggests that they may become fond of each other.

**Martinmas summer:** Indian summer (St. Martin's Day is November 11).
**coulter:** the knife of the plough.
**purlieu:** neighboring district.
*viva voce:* by voice, orally.
**spencer:** a short jacket.
**victorine:** a small cape.

QUESTION: What is the contrast between Henchard and Farfrae described in this chapter?

# CHAPTER 15

## Summary

Although Elizabeth-Jane does not wear fine clothes, she appreciates finery and is delighted when Henchard gives her a box of colored gloves. She buys a bonnet, dress and sunshade to match them, and suddenly people notice her beauty. The townspeople say that she dressed quietly before in order to emphasize this change. She is disappointed that Farfrae seems to take no notice of her. She resolves to continue to improve her education.

One of Henchard's workers, Abel Whittle, is a slow young man who has trouble waking up in the morning. When he is late, he delays the other men, and Henchard warns him that he must reform. When Whittle is late again the next morning, Henchard angrily goes to rouse the man himself. He makes Whittle come to work without his trousers, to shame him so that he will never oversleep again.

Farfrae, horrified at the sight of a workman without his proper clothes, orders Whittle to go home and dress. Henchard protests, but Farfrae threatens to resign as manager if Whittle is not allowed to dress himself properly.

A boy who arrives with a request for Farfrae to value a haystack tells Henchard that people trust and like Farfrae. Henchard is hurt that Farfrae thought him tyrannical in his treatment of Abel Whittle, and distressed by the knowledge that people prefer to deal with Farfrae rather than with him.

Henchard and Farfrae are reconciled at the end of the chapter, as Henchard agrees to let his manager value the haystack.

## Commentary

Elizabeth-Jane is disappointed that her new clothes inspire the admiration of the townspeople but apparently do not impress Farfrae. She cares about his opinion.

The conflict between Farfrae and Henchard over the treatment of Abel Whittle indicates the differences in temperament between the two. Although they become friends again after the quarrel, Hardy describes the episode as "the seed that was to lift the foundation of this friendship."

Henchard regrets that he has told Farfrae the secrets of his past. When he accuses the young man of crossing him because of that secret knowledge, Farfrae assures him that he is mistaken.

**Baruch:** the Biblical Jeremiah's scribe and disciple.
**Rochefoucauld:** a French philosopher, who believed that human conduct is motivated by selfishness.
**fretted my gizzard:** worried me.
**diment:** diamond.
*sotto voce:* under one's breath.
**scantling:** a little bit.

QUESTION: What is the significance of the fact that Henchard "had kept Abel's old mother in coals and snuff all the previous winter"?

# CHAPTER 16

## Summary
Henchard becomes more and more reserved with Farfrae, courteous rather than affectionate.

When Farfrae asks to borrow some rick cloths to make a marquee for an entertainment on a day of national celebration, Henchard realizes that, as mayor, he should plan some celebration. He makes rival plans and spends a lot of money. Farfrae arranges to charge admission. Henchard's entertainment is to be free.

Although the weather has been fine, it rains on the day of the celebrations. Henchard's entertainment on the open green is a failure, and the people flock to Farfrae's tent. Henchard watches the dancing, at first amused by the sight of Farfrae's enthusiasm, but then angry at the admiration the young man inspires. He overhears the townspeople comparing his efforts unfavorably with Farfrae's. When Elizabeth-Jane dances with Farfrae, she looks to Henchard for approval. He frowns.

When the townspeople joke about the superiority of his manager's effort, Henchard remarks that Farfrae will soon cease to be his manager. Farfrae accepts his decision.

## Commentary

The total failure of Henchard's plans and the success of Farfrae's separate the two men. We feel pity for Henchard, and also for Farfrae, who unwittingly antagonizes his master. Quick temper is apparent in Henchard's dismissal of his manager, but he is goaded by the remarks of the townspeople and by disappointment at the failure of his plans.

The chapter concentrates on the relationship between Henchard and Farfrae.

**Correggio:** fifteenth-century Italian painter.
**stunpoll:** stone head.
**randy:** (Scottish dialect) lively.

QUESTION: How do Farfrae's strength of will and intelligence affect his reaction to Henchard's impulsiveness?

# CHAPTER 17

## Summary

Elizabeth-Jane is ashamed when someone hints that her stepfather frowned because she forgot her position by dancing. When she leaves, Farfrae follows her and walks her to the town. He explains what has happened, and says that he had a question to ask her before the rift with her father made it impossible.

Elizabeth-Jane realizes that she is in love with Farfrae. She is disturbed by the prospect of his leaving Casterbridge, but Farfrae decides that Casterbridge has enough grain trade for two, and sets up his own business.

Henchard is hurt that Farfrae takes his hasty words of anger seriously. He denounces Farfrae when he learns that his former manager is setting up another wheat business. He makes Elizabeth-Jane promise not to see Farfrae, then he writes to Farfrae to tell him of this promise.

Susan wishes that Farfrae would become Henchard's son-in-law and that the two men would be friendly again, but she does not dare to suggest this.

When the two men meet in the market, Henchard does not speak.

## Commentary

The friendship between Henchard and Farfrae is broken, although Farfrae still has friendly feelings for the older man. Henchard's anger is not shared by other members of the town council, and he is isolated by his enmity toward Farfrae.

**varden:** farthing.
*modus vivendi:* way of living, working arrangement.
**Novalis:** poet and novelist.
**Padan-Aram:** Jacob's country in the Bible.
**Bellerophon:** Greek mythological hero who was punished for his pride.

QUESTION: How do the events of this chapter prove that "Character is Fate"?

# CHAPTER 18

## Summary

Susan is seriously ill, but seems to rally. Meanwhile, Henchard receives a letter from Lucetta, the woman from Jersey, in which she accepts his explanation and thanks him for the money. She asks that he meet her to return her letters. He goes to the place she names, but she does not appear.

Susan writes a note with this direction: "Mr. Michael Henchard. Not to be opened till Elizabeth-Jane's wedding-day." One night, while Elizabeth-Jane is sitting with her, Susan confesses that she had written notes to her and to Farfrae summoning them to the granary in order that they might be alone together. She had hoped they would marry.

Susan dies one Sunday morning.

## Commentary

Susan's death is announced in reply to Farfrae's inquiry at the house. His concern for the family is not ended by Henchard's anger.

Suspense is created by the letter from Lucetta and by her failure to meet Henchard to receive her letters. Another source of mystery is Susan's note to Henchard with instructions to delay its opening until Elizabeth-Jane's wedding day.

Elizabeth-Jane's thoughts as she sits in the darkness beside her dying mother show the growth of her character. She reflects on life and fate.

The gossip among the townspeople at the end of the chapter provides some comic relief after the somber events.

**skellintons:** skeletons.

QUESTION: What does Lucetta's letter indicate about her character?

# CHAPTER 19

## Summary

In his loneliness, Henchard reveals to Elizabeth-Jane that he is her real father. He does not confess that he sold Susan to Newson. Elizabeth-Jane is confused, but agrees that she should take Henchard's name.

While looking for documents to prove what he has said, Henchard accidentally opens and reads the letter Susan wrote while she was dying. The letter reveals that his daughter died shortly after their separation, and that Elizabeth-Jane is Newson's daughter.

Henchard is overcome. He walks alone all night in the darkness by the river, near the ruined priory and the gallows. He is greeted at breakfast by Elizabeth-Jane's kiss and by her acceptance of him as her father. The joy he had looked for is gone. He cannot rejoice in his connection with Newson's daughter.

## Commentary

In this chapter, Hardy makes use of setting to reflect mood. Henchard's despair and pain find an appropriate backdrop in the gloom and darkness of the river and the priory.

The chance opening of Susan's letter destroys Henchard's hopes for happiness. There is irony in the fact that his confession to Elizabeth-Jane causes the discovery of the note, for he looks through his papers in order to convince her of the truth of what he says. Henchard feels that some fate is controlling him and destroying any possibility of happiness.

**pier-glass:** mirror.
**Prester John:** mythological king who was condemned to have his food snatched away by harpies, half-woman, half-bird crea-

tures, because of his presumptuous attempt to rule Paradise.

**Schwarzwasser:** black water, the name of a Polish river.
**weir:** dam.


QUESTION: How will the revelation that Elizabeth-Jane is not his daughter affect Henchard's behavior? Why?


# CHAPTER 20

## Summary
Henchard is cold toward Elizabeth-Jane and shows emotion only when correcting her for using dialect, or criticizing her handwriting.

She tries to please him, but her kindness in bringing food to one of the workers, Nance Mockridge, annoys him. When Nance says that Elizabeth-Jane served at the Three Mariners when she and her mother first came to Casterbridge, Henchard grows angry.

At the same time, he learns that he is not to be chosen as an alderman when his term as mayor ends. The council intends to choose Farfrae.

While visiting her mother's grave one morning, Elizabeth-Jane sees a well-dressed young woman also visiting the spot. When she sees her again another day, and the woman is kind to her, Elizabeth-Jane confesses her unhappiness. The woman proposes that Elizabeth-Jane be her companion in her new house in Casterbridge.

Henchard writes a note to Farfrae, giving him permission to court Elizabeth-Jane. He is disturbed by her presence in the house.

## Commentary
The details of Henchard's dislike for Elizabeth-Jane show the difficulties of the girl's position. We feel sympathy for her, and for her ignorance of the cause of Henchard's changed feelings.

The woman who meets Elizabeth-Jane in the graveyard gives her a promise of escape. Her identity is a mystery.

Elizabeth-Jane's reaction to the sight of Farfrae indicates that she loves him, but his feelings about her are not obvious.

Henchard's desire to be rid of his stepdaughter, by marrying her to his enemy, may bring the two together.

**jowned;** jolted.
**Minerva:** Roman goddess of wisdom.
**Princess Ida:** the heroine of Tennyson's poem, "The Princess."
**wimbling:** boring a hole.
**the Constantines:** Roman emperors, father and son.
**Karnac:** an ancient Egyptian city on the Nile.
**Austerlitz:** where Napoleon defeated the Russians in 1805. After this battle, Napoleon's fortunes began to decline.

QUESTION: Why does the stranger offer to help Elizabeth-Jane?

# CHAPTER 21

## Summary

Elizabeth-Jane watches eagerly as High-Place Hall is prepared for its new mistress, the woman she met in the graveyard. She sees Henchard also come to look at the house.

Later, when Elizabeth-Jane asks her stepfather if he would consent to her leaving home, he agrees. The next day she again meets the woman, whose name is Miss Templeman. She asks Elizabeth-Jane to come to her that evening.

Henchard feels some remorse when Elizabeth-Jane packs and leaves so suddenly. He is touched by the signs of industry and care in her room, but he can find no words to express his feelings.

## Commentary

When Elizabeth-Jane leaves, Henchard is completely alone. He regrets his solitude. The chance for an independent life cheers Elizabeth-Jane and gives her strength.

The stranger has some connection with Henchard, as he visits her house.

Hardy's interest in architecture is apparent in his description of High-Place Hall. The grotesque details of the house provide a background for Miss Templeman's activities.

**Palladian:** a formal, neo-classical, grandiose style of architecture.

QUESTION: How does Henchard's conduct with Elizabeth-Jane compare with his treatment of other characters in the novel?

## CHAPTER 22

**Summary**

The chapter begins with a flashback to the previous evening to explain Henchard's visit to High-Place Hall. He had received a letter from Lucetta, who has inherited money and has come to live in Casterbridge after hearing of Susan's death. She has taken the name of her benefactor, Templeman. That is why, when Henchard had asked for "Miss Le Sueur," her previous name, he was turned away. After receiving another note, Henchard calls, and is told that Miss Templeman is busy. He decides to delay calling for several days.

Elizabeth-Jane and Lucetta become friendly. Lucetta tells Elizabeth-Jane that her home is Jersey, although she has announced on arriving in Casterbridge that she comes from Bath.

When Henchard fails to repeat his call, Lucetta watches the marketplace and sees him there. Elizabeth-Jane watches too, and looks so intently when she sees Farfrae that Lucetta asks whom she looks at. Elizabeth-Jane, avoiding a direct answer, identifies many people.

After Elizabeth-Jane confides that her stepfather dislikes her, Lucetta wonders if Elizabeth-Jane's presence may be preventing Henchard from calling. She sends Elizabeth-Jane on an errand and writes a note to Henchard to tell him of the opportunity.

When Lucetta hears a man's step on the stairs, she hides in the curtains. When she jumps out, however, she sees not Henchard but another man.

**Commentary**

The surprise of the chapter's ending holds our attention, and Lucetta's action shows her childishness.

Henchard seems to feel only duty and the possibility of material gain in his decision to marry Lucetta.

The location of High-Place Hall opposite the marketplace gives the women a view of the proceedings and of the men who interest them.

**weak Apostle:** Peter, who denied knowing Jesus.

*mon ami:* my friend.

*étourderie:* thoughtlessness.

**carrefour:** crossroads.

**Titian:** sixteenth-century Venetian painter.

**gibbous:** rounded.

**cyma-recta:** an architectural term for a line curved outward, then inward.

**Candlemas:** February 2.

QUESTION: What do we learn about Lucetta's character in this chapter?

# CHAPTER 23

## Summary

The man who enters the room is Farfrae, elegantly dressed, and Lucetta is immediately impressed. He has called to see Elizabeth-Jane. Instead of telling him that Elizabeth-Jane will be out for several hours, Lucetta says that she is expected back any minute, and persuades Farfrae to wait.

Farfrae has called because of Henchard's note, giving him permission to court his daughter. After an embarrassing silence, he talks to Lucetta about his business. His enthusiasm attracts her.

They overhear a difficult business transaction in the market below, and Farfrae goes down to intervene. His sympathy and humane dealings impress Lucetta further. She praises him and invites him to visit again. Farfrae leaves, having forgotten that he had come to see Elizabeth-Jane.

A few minutes after Farfrae's departure, Henchard calls, in response to Lucetta's note. She refuses to see him, saying that she has a headache. She now hopes to keep Elizabeth-Jane with her as protection from Henchard's attentions.

## Commentary

Lucetta and Farfrae are mutually attracted. Lucetta is something of a flirt, and Farfrae responds to her flirting. She deceives her visitor about Elizabeth-Jane's absence. She also plans to continue the deception by ignoring Henchard, whom she is bound to marry, so that she may see Farfrae without restraint.

The irony of the situation, as Farfrae arrives to court Eliza-

36

beth-Jane and becomes involved with Lucetta, is apparent. Elizabeth-Jane is again the victim of forces beyond her control. Her prospects for happiness are clouded again.

**kerseymere:** fine wool.
**St. Helier:** a large town, capital of Jersey.
**Lady-day:** March 25.
**Dan:** Sir.

QUESTION: What will be the effects of a love affair between Lucetta and Farfrae?

# CHAPTER 24

## Summary
The two women wait for Saturday, market day, so that they may watch the activity in the market place. Without knowing it, they both watch for the same man, Farfrae.

One day, a strange machine appears in the market place. It is a seed drill. Farfrae has arranged for its purchase and understands it, while Henchard is openly scornful of the new machine.

Elizabeth-Jane notices something in the way Lucetta and Farfrae greet each other, and watches her companion carefully. She recognizes that Lucetta is in love with Farfrae.

Lucetta discusses her past entanglement with Henchard with Elizabeth-Jane, without revealing the identities of the people involved. She hopes that Elizabeth-Jane will assure her of her freedom. Elizabeth-Jane guesses that Lucetta's story is not about a friend, as she says, but about herself. She refuses to make a judgment on the situation.

## Commentary
Lucetta's concern for her wardrobe stands in contrast to Elizabeth-Jane's careful modesty in dressing. Her open flirting with Farfrae contrasts with Elizabeth-Jane's shyness and desire to win Farfrae's approval by improving her mind.

Henchard's reaction to the seed drill emphasizes his conservatism. Elizabeth-Jane's lament that the "romance of the sower is gone" shows her awareness of change and her recognition of the loss involved in progress. The changes brought by the use of machines begin to affect Casterbridge.

Our sympathy for Elizabeth-Jane grows as she seems destined to be unhappy.

**Heptarchy:** the seven Saxon kingdoms.

QUESTION: How has Elizabeth-Jane's character changed since she left Henchard's house?

## CHAPTER 25

### Summary
When Farfrae calls on Lucetta, she insists that Elizabeth-Jane be present too. As Elizabeth-Jane watches the two, she realizes that Farfrae's attraction to her has been displaced by a passion for Lucetta.

Henchard also calls. He proposes marriage, but Lucetta delays answering. Henchard and Farfrae continue to call.

Elizabeth-Jane admires Lucetta's beauty and is not surprised that Farfrae prefers that beauty to hers. She grieves at the loss of Farfrae's love. She is also upset by Henchard's complete indifference to her. She knows of no way in which she has injured him, so cannot understand his treatment of her.

### Commentary
The rival lovers direct their attentions to Lucetta, but the action is seen through Elizabeth-Jane's eyes. Thus, we are constantly aware of the pain she is feeling. Elizabeth-Jane's stoic reaction to her suffering does not diminish her pain.

QUESTION: Does Lucetta's cry, "I won't be a slave to the past," inspire our sympathy? How does her attitude relate to the rest of the novel?

## CHAPTER 26

### Summary
Henchard and Farfrae meet by chance, and Henchard speaks to his former manager about the unidentified woman in his past. He says that he has offered to marry her, and she has refused. Farfrae agrees that Henchard owes the woman nothing more. The two men part. Henchard does not tell Farfrae that the woman is Lucetta.

While Henchard is visiting Lucetta, Farfrae also calls. During the visit, Lucetta makes her preference for the younger man clear.

Henchard is angry that his rivalry with Farfrae in business has extended to a rivalry in love. He sends for Jopp, the man who would have been his manager had Farfrae not appeared. Henchard hires him and explicitly states his enmity for Farfrae.

In an attempt to outdo his rival, Henchard secretly consults a weather prophet, Mr. Fall, about the harvest weather. He then buys grain in great quantities, only to have to sell at a loss when the weather changes. In his anger, he fires Jopp for failing to restrain his purchasing. Jopp is angry and vows to avenge himself on Henchard.

## Commentary

The visit to the weather prophet is Henchard's attempt to find a basis for action. He is superstitious, while Farfrae is scientific.

The portrait of the prophet is psychologically realistic and endearing, but Henchard's reliance on his information leads to financial ruin. After Farfrae's description to Lucetta of the success that results from being satisfied with small profits, Henchard's speculation on a vast scale seems doomed to failure.

*pis aller:* last resource; worst.
**Alastor:** Greek mythological spirit of revenge.
**water-tights:** boots.
**the evil:** scrofula, tuberculosis.
**dungmixen:** dunghill.

QUESTION: Why does Hardy have Henchard visit the weather prophet, Mr. Fall, rather than simply guessing wrong about the weather?

## CHAPTER 27

### Summary

Farfrae begins buying grain as the promise of a good harvest drives the price down. Then the weather changes and the price soars. Henchard sees that if he had waited, his grain would have been worth double what he paid for it. He feels that he is the victim of "some power . . . working against him."

The collision of two hay wagons, one Farfrae's and one

Henchard's, in the road outside Lucetta's house brings Henchard to the scene. He settles the matter, then he calls at Lucetta's, but she refuses to see him. He waits and sees her go out with Farfrae. Following them in the dark, he overhears their declarations of love.

Henchard returns to Lucetta's house and waits for her return. When he threatens to reveal the past if she refuses to marry him, Lucetta faints. Then she agrees to the marriage.

Elizabeth-Jane is angry with Henchard for his harsh treatment of Lucetta, but she is baffled by the power he seems to have over her friend.

## Commentary

Henchard's feeling that "some power" is against him shows his superstitious nature. He does not analyze the causes of his failures to see where and how far he is responsible for what happens. He is angry at Farfrae's good fortune and resolves to force Lucetta to marry him so that Farfrae will not be the victor in both business and love. He does not examine his motives for insisting on the marriage.

**zwailing:** swaying.
**gawk-hammer:** awkward, dimless.

QUESTION: Why does Lucetta agree to marry Henchard when Farfrae has declared his love for her?

## CHAPTER 28

### Summary

As magistrate, Henchard presides at the trial of an old woman charged with disorderly behavior. After the constable has spoken, the woman is allowed to defend herself. She tells the court that 20 years ago, at Weydon-Priors Fair, she saw a man sell his wife. She then points at Henchard and identifies him as the man, saying that, because of that act, he has no right to judge her.

Henchard recognizes the woman as the furmity seller. He doesn't deny her story, and leaves the court.

Lucetta hears the story and regrets bitterly that she must marry such a man. She walks to the Ring and doesn't return until dark. Then she goes to Port-Bredy for a few days. When she returns to Casterbridge, she is out walking along the road to Port-Bredy when Henchard calls.

## Commentary
Henchard's past is no longer hidden. He makes no attempt to discredit the old woman's story, although he could easily deny it, and point to the contrast between her status and his own respectability. He has a sense of the moral justice of what has happened and now has the strength to bear the shame of his past.

Chance is important again, as the old woman appears and recognizes Henchard after 20 years. Hardy makes the coincidence probable by suggesting Henchard's own readiness for the revelation. He is willing to bear the burden of his shame. He is learning stoic resignation through the loss of happiness and through failure.

**Shallow and Silence:** comic characters who act as justices of the peace in *Henry IV, Part I*.
**ashlar:** square stone used in building.
**Hannah Dominy:** anno domini (A.D.)
**wambling:** weaving.
**turmit-hit:** turnip-head.
**larry:** commotion.

QUESTION: Why is it important that the furmity woman accuses Henchard while he is sitting as a judge rather than while he is at home or in the street?

# CHAPTER 29

## Summary
Lucetta has walked a mile out of town when Elizabeth-Jane joins her. They are chased by a ferocious bull that has escaped on the way to market. They run to a barn, but the animal gets inside and chases them back and forth. Henchard appears, subdues the bull and takes the hysterical Lucetta home.

When Elizabeth-Jane returns to the barn for Lucetta's muff, she meets Farfrae driving into Casterbridge and rides with him. She tells him what has happened. After taking her home, Farfrae goes to his lodgings, where his belongings are being packed.

When Lucetta recovers, Henchard tries to comfort her by

saying that he will not insist on an immediate marriage. Lucetta confesses that she cannot marry him because she has married Farfrae in Port-Bredy. Henchard's chief creditor, Mr. Grower, was a witness to the ceremony. Henchard's hope that the prospect of his marriage to Lucetta would restore his credit is disappointed.

Henchard is furious that Lucetta has broken her word to him. Lucetta offers to lend him money, but he angrily refuses.

## Commentary

The chance appearance of the furmity woman leads to the marriage of Lucetta and Farfrae. The secrecy of the ceremony protects Lucetta from Henchard. She fears marriage to a man who could sell his wife, and she fears that Farfrae would not want to marry her if he knew of her past relationship with Henchard.

The violence of the episode with the bull seems appropriate to the urgency of Lucetta's actions and to the doom that Henchard himself fears. Henchard's action in saving Lucetta and Elizabeth-Jane is ironic. He takes great care to rescue the woman who is already his rival's wife, and he almost completely ignores the stepdaughter whose love will be his only comfort in the future.

**Yahoo:** degraded creature in the form of a man in Jonathan Swift's *Gulliver's Travels*.
**Thames Tunnel:** completed in 1843.
**Gurth's collar:** brass collar worn by a swineherd in Sir Walter Scott's *Ivanhoe* as a sign of his bondage.

QUESTION: Why is the episode of the bull introduced? Is it effective?

# CHAPTER 30

## Summary

Farfrae prepares to move to High-Place Hall. Before confessing her secret marriage, Lucetta tries to get Elizabeth-Jane's approval by referring again to the story of the woman with two lovers. However, Elizabeth-Jane knows that Lucetta has recently promised to marry her first lover, Henchard. When she discovers that Lucetta has secretly married Farfrae instead, she is horrified. She decides to leave the house at once.

## Commentary
Elizabeth-Jane, concerned about propriety, thinks that Lucetta ought to marry Henchard because of her past behavior and her promise. She, like Lucetta, loves Farfrae and had hoped that he would love her. Lucetta's attempt to have her friend stay on in the house fails, because Elizabeth-Jane disapproves of the marriage for these two reasons. She moves out of the house the very night that Farfrae moves in, and shows strength of character in taking lodgings on her own.

**John Gilpin:** the hero of William Cowper's ballad, "John Gilpin's Ride."

**Ovid:** Latin poet. The line is from his *Metamorphoses*: "I see better things, and approve, but follow worse."

**Nathan:** the prophet who condemned David's marriage to Bathsheba.

QUESTION: Why is Elizabeth-Jane so concerned with propriety, in view of her own background?

# CHAPTER 31

## Summary
Henchard has lost his reputation for respectability through the furmity woman's report. In financial difficulty, he is forced to declare himself bankrupt. In his desire to deal justly with his creditors, he offers even his watch to them. They are moved by the gesture, and refuse to strip him of everything. He immediately sells the watch and takes the money to the poorest of the people to whom he is in debt.

Elizabeth-Jane takes lodgings and tries to get in touch with Henchard. He does not answer her letters or meet her in the streets. He moves into rooms in Jopp's cottage, near the Priory Mill where he had wandered the night he discovered that Elizabeth-Jane was not his daughter. He retreats to the poorest and most disreputable section of Casterbridge.

## Commentary
Henchard falls as Farfrae rises. In his descent, Henchard acts with honor and compassion. His decision to take rooms in

Jopp's cottage suggests his despair, for the gloomy setting near the river echoes his own gloom.

Elizabeth-Jane seeks her stepfather to comfort him. He refuses to see her because he feels that he has no right to comfort or affection. He is obsessed by the shame of his double failure, in business and in love.

QUESTION: What is Henchard's reaction to the lowest point of his fortunes? How does his reaction indicate the complexity of his character?

# CHAPTER 32

## Summary

Henchard often stands on the bridge frequented by the town's failures. Jopp finds him there one day, and tells him that Farfrae has bought his house and furniture. Later, Farfrae drives by, and asks Henchard about a rumor that he plans to emigrate. He asks Henchard to stay in Casterbridge and suggests that Henchard take lodgings in his old house, with whatever he might like of his own furniture. Henchard refuses the offer, but is touched by Farfrae's generosity.

When Henchard falls ill, Elizabeth-Jane goes to him and nurses him. He recovers health and strength in her care. He applies to Farfrae for work, and is hired as a laborer. He continues to wear the black suit, now ragged, that he wore as a gentleman instead of clothes appropriate to a laboring job.

One day, the townspeople announce that Henchard has "busted out drinking after taking nothing for twenty-one years!"

## Commentary

Henchard is influenced by two contrasting characters. Jopp, who hates both Farfrae and Henchard, taunts the ex-mayor with his failure and emphasizes the success of his former manager. On the other hand, Farfrae tries to help his former employer, treating him with generous consideration by offering him lodging and the gift of any furniture that might have sentimental value.

Elizabeth-Jane is another influence. Under her affectionate care, Henchard recovers strength and some hope. Her kindness in nursing him has a positive influence, while Lucetta's past care was a source of pain.

Henchard's anticipation of the day when his oath of abstinence will end shows that he looks forward to escaping from his troubles in drink, and gives promise of trouble.

QUESTION: What is the significance of Henchard's clothing?

# CHAPTER 33

## Summary

At the Three Mariners one Sunday, Henchard sees Farfrae and Lucetta pass after church. He has been drinking, and insists that the choir sing a psalm cursing the man of "ill-got riches." He announces to everyone that the curse is on Farfrae.

Henchard resents the pity with which Abel Whittle looks at him when they work together, so Elizabeth-Jane offers to take Whittle's place. She also takes tea to Henchard in an effort to prevent his drinking at the inn.

Lucetta is always with her husband and comes across Henchard at work. She did not know that Farfrae had hired Henchard. She is embarrassed by the encounter, which Henchard makes more difficult by his remarks about the distance between her class and his own.

Lucetta sends Henchard a letter, asking him not to make such comments when they chance to meet. Henchard mocks her for sending a note that could be used to reveal their past relationship, but he destroys the document.

Elizabeth-Jane sees Henchard and Farfrae together on the top floor of the granary one day and notices the look of hatred in her stepfather's face. She decides that she must warn Farfrae.

## Commentary

Henchard's heavy drinking increases his hatred for Farfrae and his resentment of his own situation. With the passage of time, Farfrae comes to regard Henchard as an ordinary workman, which angers Henchard further.

Elizabeth-Jane's terror at the sight of Henchard's hatred for Farfrae is an important preparation for future events.

**Stonehenge:** a great ring of ancient standing stones in Wiltshire, England.
**rantipole:** rough, boisterous.

**Rosalind:** heroine of Shakespeare's play *As You Like It*.

QUESTION: Why is Henchard's sarcasm when he meets Lucetta appropriate?

# CHAPTER 34

## Summary

Elizabeth-Jane warns Farfrae about Henchard's hatred and threats. He is not alarmed, but later hears from others about Henchard's anger. He is advised by his fellow council members to drop his plan to set up Henchard in a seed shop. When he tells the shop owner of the council's decision, the man is disappointed and tells Henchard that Farfrae is responsible for the decision not to buy the shop.

Farfrae tells Lucetta of Henchard's enmity and Lucetta advises that they move away. Farfrae agrees. However, when the current mayor dies, Farfrae is offered the position. He accepts.

Lucetta meets Henchard by chance and asks him to return her letters. He remembers that the package of her letters is still in the safe at his old house. He obtains permission to collect them, intending to read the letters aloud to Farfrae. He does read them, but omits the signature. He finds that he cannot take the revenge that he had planned.

## Commentary

Henchard's bitterness is increased by the incident of the seed shop. He does not know the actual facts of the situation. It is ironic that Henchard blames Farfrae when Farfrae was the instigator of the plan in the first place and only retreated at the urging of the other council members.

Henchard plans to expose Lucetta's past to her husband by reading her letters. In spite of the drinking he has done, he finds that he cannot read Lucetta's name out to Farfrae. He is not callous or cruel enough for such revenge.

Farfrae, as mayor, has completely taken over Henchard's position in the town.

**Tamerlane:** the famous Mongol leader described in Marlowe's
   *Tamberlaine*.
**Aphrodite:** Greek goddess of love.

QUESTION: How is the situation of Henchard's reading of Lucetta's letters made dramatic?

# CHAPTER 35

**Summary**

A flashback shows that Lucetta overheard Henchard reading her letters aloud to Farfrae. She is amazed when she realizes that her husband has learned nothing of her past from the reading.

She writes again to Henchard, and asks him to meet her at the Ring after he has finished the next day's work. Lucetta's obvious distress and the memory of Susan's suffering causes Henchard to have pity. He promises to return the letters.

**Commentary**

Hardy uses a parallel in setting to link events in the novel. Henchard's reunion with Susan and his meeting with Lucetta occur at the same place. The fact of Susan's suffering because of his action makes Henchard want to save Lucetta from similar pain.

His generosity is admirable, and his sense of responsibility contrasts with Lucetta's own irresponsible actions.

QUESTION: Why is Lucetta's haggard appearance important?

# CHAPTER 36

**Summary**

Henchard gives Jopp the package of Lucetta's letters to return. Jopp has reason to hate Lucetta because she refused to speak to Farfrae to secure the manager's job for him. Jopp has been in Jersey, and speculates about the relationship between Lucetta and Henchard. Instead of delivering the letters, he opens the package and reads them. Then he pauses on his way to Lucetta's house and drinks at Peter's Finger, an inn in Mixen Lane, in the disreputable part of Casterbridge. Jopp reads the letters aloud, and Nance Mockridge remarks that they offer good material for a skimmity ride.

A stranger looking for the way into Casterbridge passes by and contributes money for the expense of such a ride. Jopp delivers the parcel to Lucetta in the morning. She immediately burns the letters.

## Commentary

Jopp's evening at Peter's Finger gives the townspeople an opportunity for humiliating Lucetta. The letters had been read aloud by Henchard without harming Lucetta, but Jopp's reading brings disaster to her.

The description of Mixen Lane and its inhabitants reveals the seamy side of Casterbridge in vivid detail. Hardy uses the darkness and secrecy of the place as an appropriate beginning for the exposure of Lucetta's past.

The entry of a stranger creates suspense.

**mixen:** (dialect) dung.
**Adullam:** hiding place for people in trouble.
**skittle alley:** bowling alley.
**Ashton, Ravenswood:** in Scott's *The Bride of Lammermoor,* Ashton sees Ravenswood disappear into quicksand.
**swingels:** cudgels.
**skimmity ride:** skimmington ride, a rowdy procession intended to make fun of a man whose wife is shrewish or unfaithful.
**get it in train:** get it started.

QUESTION: What is the significance of the appearance of the stranger in Mixen Lane?

## CHAPTER 37

### Summary

There is great excitement in the town about a "Royal Personage," who is to pass through Casterbridge. Farfrae and the town council plan a celebration, in which Henchard asks to participate. Farfrae and the council refuse his request.

At the moment when Farfrae is about to welcome the royal carriage, Henchard steps in front of him and waves a rough flag. There is a disturbance as Farfrae pushes him aside. Everyone is shocked, but the royal guest pretends not to have noticed anything unusual.

After the incident, Henchard overhears Lucetta telling some women companions that Henchard had nothing to do with her husband's success. She does not give credit to Henchard for giving Farfrae a start, partly because she doesn't know the real circumstances of the past, and partly because she wants to forget Henchard.

The townspeople talk about the skimmity ride. Jopp is the main instigator. He wants to humiliate Farfrae and Lucetta, who have had such a triumph in the day's celebrations.

## Commentary

Henchard refuses to act sensibly, and forces his way to the front of the crowd with his flag to welcome the royal visitor. He is not acting maliciously, but in anger at the council's refusal to recognize that he has some right to participate in public affairs. He has lost his wealth and public office, but he served the town loyally in the past.

Farfrae's rough treatment of Henchard is justified by the circumstances, but the public insult will increase Henchard's anger.

Lucetta's comments show that she is callous and indifferent to Henchard's feelings. She is also ready to lie and eager to forget the past.

The plans for the skimmity ride are mentioned at the end of the chapter to cast a shadow over the success that Lucetta and Farfrae enjoy.

*fête carillonée*: (French) festival with bells.
**Calpurnia:** Julius Caesar's loyal wife.
**go snacks wi'en:** eat at his table, share.
**toppered:** shamed.
**hontish:** proud.

QUESTION: What effect will the skimmity ride have on Lucetta?

# CHAPTER 38

## Summary

Henchard is stunned by Lucetta's words and by Farfrae's violence. Jopp taunts him with his fallen state and confides his own hatred for the pair. Henchard seeks no allies in revenge and ignores Jopp. He leaves a message at Farfrae's house and goes to wait for his former friend on the top floor of the granary, where Elizabeth-Jane had seen him with Farfrae once before. He plans to fight Farfrae. To make the fight fair, he binds one of his arms behind him.

When Farfrae comes in answer to Henchard's summons, he is humming a song that he had sung at the Three Mariners on the day that the two men met. Henchard is moved by the sound and by the memory of their friendship. Although he fights Farfrae fiercely, he cannot bring himself to throw the younger man out of the window, as he had planned. Instead, he lets Farfrae go and lies down in despair in a corner of the loft.

Farfrae doesn't return home, but goes off in answer to a summons from Weatherbury, although he had planned to go to Budmouth. Henchard hears the change of plans and sees that Farfrae does not immediately summon justice against him.

He wanders to the lonely bridge, where he hears a confusion of noise in the town.

## Commentary

Henchard has attempted to kill Farfrae, but his hatred is not murderous and he cannot bring himself to destroy the man who was once his friend. His affection for Farfrae and his memories of their friendship, revived by the song Farfrae hums, prevent him from taking the final step of his revenge.

Farfrae goes on, not to Budmouth as he had planned, but to Weatherbury. Only Henchard and Abel Whittle, to whom Farfrae speaks, know of this change in plans.

Hardy describes the fight in the granary immediately after the triumph of Farfrae's public career to emphasize the danger such triumph involves. Farfrae escapes only because of Henchard's generosity. Triumph and disaster are juxtaposed.

**Weltlust:** worldly pleasure.
**fiere:** friend (the song is "Auld Lang Syne").

QUESTION: What will Farfrae's reaction to Henchard's attack be?

## CHAPTER 39

### Summary

Solomon Longways and other of Farfrae's men sent the

anonymous note asking Farfrae to visit Weatherby, to protect him from sight of the skimmity ride.

Lucetta waits at home for Farfrae's return and hears the noise of the skimmity ride. She is disturbed in the midst of her comfortable surroundings, where she feels secure. She has burned Henchard's letters and has had great success as the mayor's wife. Thus, the shock of the skimmity ride is unexpected.

Lucetta hears her servants describing the figures in the procession. Although Elizabeth-Jane comes to try to prevent her from seeing the display, Lucetta insists on looking. She is overcome by the sight of the effigies of Henchard and her tied back to back on a donkey. She falls down in an epileptic seizure. A doctor is called and, worried by her reaction, he orders that Farfrae be sent for at once.

Meanwhile, one of the citizens, Mr. Grower, hears the noise and summons the police. When they reach the main street, however, there is no sign of any disturbance. They go to Peter's Finger and find all the participants in the skimmity ride sitting quietly drinking beer. They can find out nothing from "this mute and inoffensive assembly."

## Commentary

Lucetta's disgrace immediately follows the height of her triumph and shatters her confidence that she has nothing to fear. Her epileptic attack is a surprise because no mention of the disease has been made previously, but her pregnancy may be responsible for the reaction.

Elizabeth-Jane attempts to protect her friend, even though she herself has condemned Lucetta for marrying Farfrae when she was committed to marrying Henchard.

The ruse to prevent Farfrae from seeing the skimmity ride shows how popular he is with his men.

**mummery:** performance without words.
**puce:** dark brown.
*felo de se:* (Latin) suicide.
*Comus:* a masque by Milton, in which Comus' companions disappear without a trace.

QUESTION: Is the effect of the skimmity ride foreseen by those who plan it?

# CHAPTER 40

## Summary

When Henchard hears the noise of the skimmity ride, he does not let it disturb his thoughts. At home, he learns that Elizabeth-Jane has gone to Mrs. Farfrae's. He follows her there and learns what has happened.

When told that men have been sent to meet Farfrae on the Budmouth Road, Henchard says that Farfrae has gone not to Budmouth but to Weatherby. No one will believe him after his unruly behavior of the morning, so he goes to seek Farfrae himself.

Henchard meets Farfrae, who refuses to believe him when he tells of Lucetta's sudden illness. Farfrae continues on his way, and Henchard is desolate. He returns to Casterbridge and talks to Elizabeth-Jane about Lucetta's condition. He is moved by Elizabeth-Jane's affectionate welcome and, as he returns to his lodgings, resolves to ask his stepdaughter to live with him.

Jopp tells Henchard that a sea captain has been asking to see him, but Henchard goes to bed without taking any interest in the fact.

When Farfrae returns to Casterbridge hours later, he is appalled by Lucetta's condition. He sits up with her for the rest of the night. Before morning, Lucetta dies.

## Commentary

When Henchard is rejected by his fellow men for his behavior, he "loses his self-respect, the last mental prop under poverty." He sincerely wants to help Lucetta and Farfrae, but can find no one to believe what he says.

He discovers in this chapter "a pin-point of light" in Elizabeth-Jane's affection for him. He recognizes a bond between himself and his stepdaughter, for they both care for Lucetta and Farfrae's happiness, although they both have been injured by the marriage.

Jopp's mention of the sea captain is a source of suspense. The fact that Jopp tells of the man's arrival suggests that the stranger poses a threat to Henchard.

Lucetta's death is announced in response to Henchard's inquiry at the house, just as Susan's death was announced in answer to Farfrae's question. The parallel shows how both Farfrae and Henchard continue to care for each other, in spite of the break between them.

**Lucifer:** the morning star.

QUESTION: How is the sea captain's arrival important?

# CHAPTER 41

## Summary

Elizabeth-Jane comes to Henchard's lodgings after Lucetta's death. He is kind and sympathetic, and insists that she rest while he prepares breakfast. She falls asleep and Henchard quietly keeps the kettle boiling.

While Elizabeth-Jane is sleeping, the sea captain returns. It is Newson. Henchard is affected by the sight: his "face and eyes seemed to die." He fears that Elizabeth-Jane will not love him because of her father's return. Newson has learned that Susan is dead, and asks about Elizabeth-Jane. Unable to stop himself, Henchard says that Elizabeth-Jane is dead too. Newson is shocked by the news and leaves almost immediately. Henchard, stunned by what he has done, expects Newson to return to challenge his lie. He goes out and sees Newson get into a coach and leave Casterbridge without discovering that his daughter is alive.

Henchard and Elizabeth-Jane have breakfast together. Henchard does not feel confident enough to ask Elizabeth-Jane to come to live with him, but she promises to visit him the next morning.

Henchard is in despair at what he has done. At night, he walks beside the river and thinks of suicide. At the moment when he is about to plunge into the black water, he sees a body in the water that looks like his own. He thinks the sight a miracle, and brings Elizabeth-Jane to the weir to see what he has seen. They discover that the body is the effigy used in the skimmity ride.

Elizabeth-Jane is moved by her stepfather's loneliness. Henchard asks her if she can forgive his rough treatment of her and she assures him that she has forgotten it. They arrange to live together, and Henchard seems to come to life.

## Commentary

The mystery of the sea captain's identity is solved when he

53

reveals that he is Newson. Just as Henchard has begun to feel like a father toward Elizabeth-Jane and to hope that he may win her affection, Elizabeth-Jane's real father returns.

The irony is strong. Henchard's lie about Elizabeth-Jane's death is unpremeditated. He speaks without thinking, but is unable to follow Newson and tell him the truth because he needs to cling to Elizabeth-Jane. He has found affection and wants desperately to keep it.

Henchard is stopped from committing suicide by the sight of the effigy of himself floating in the river. He feels that the coincidence is providential. When he shows Elizabeth-Jane, she is so distressed at the thought of his committing suicide that she asks to live with him: the father and stepdaughter are brought together by the remnant of the skimmity ride.

Elizabeth-Jane's effect on Henchard is dramatic. He begins to take care of himself, to shave, change his linen and comb his hair. He says, ''even I be in Somebody's hand.''

QUESTION: What is the significance of Henchard's longing for music at the lowest point of his despair?

# CHAPTER 42

## Summary

Henchard is haunted by fear of Newson's return. His optimism fades. He lives quietly with Elizabeth-Jane, taking care of her. The town council buys a seed shop to give Henchard a new start, and he and Elizabeth-Jane manage it together. A year passes after Lucetta's death and Newson's appearance.

Farfrae learns about the skimmity ride, but conquers his desire to take revenge on those responsible. He knows that Lucetta's past is best forgotten — she had confessed, before her death, about her relationship with Henchard.

With the passage of time, Farfrae begins to understand the limits of his love for Lucetta. He knows that the knowlege of his wife's past would have come to him and that their happiness would have been shaken.

Elizabeth-Jane begins to see Farfrae without Henchard's knowledge. The two take long walks together, and one day Henchard sees Farfrae kiss Elizabeth-Jane. He is jealous, fearing what will happen if the two marry. He and Farfrae continue to avoid each other.

## Commentary

Farfrae's grief at Lucetta's death is diminished by time and by his regret about her past. He avoids Henchard but gradually comes to love Elizabeth-Jane. Her strength and modesty are a contrast to Lucetta's character.

Henchard is so dependent on Elizabeth-Jane and her affection that he fears her marriage to Farfrae. He wonders if Farfrae would still love Elizabeth-Jane if he knew that she is Susan's child by the sailor, Newson. He immediately rejects the idea of revealing Elizabeth-Jane's parentage. He laments, "Why should I still be subject to these visitations of the devil, when I try so hard to keep him away?" He does not act impulsively, restraining his jealous feelings.

**Juno's bird:** the peacock, a symbol of pride and vanity.
**Argus:** a Greek mythological creature with 100 eyes.
*solicitus timor:* (Latin) anxious fear.
*locus standi:* (Latin) a place for standing, an accepted position.

QUESTION: What picture of Farfrae is suggested in this chapter?

## CHAPTER 43

### Summary

The townspeople gossip that Farfrae and Elizabeth-Jane plan to be married. They approve of the match, and are eager to see Elizabeth-Jane raised to a higher social position.

Elizabeth-Jane and Farfrae do not speak to Henchard about their plans. He feels bitter about this, imagining what will happen to him after their marriage. He goes out one day to watch Elizabeth-Jane and Farfrae through his telescope, but sees Newson instead. When he returns home, Elizabeth-Jane tells him of a strange letter that she has received, asking her to come to the Budmouth Road or to Farfrae's house. Newson had been on the Budmouth Road, so Henchard knows that the letter is from Elizabeth-Jane's father.

Henchard advises Elizabeth-Jane to go to Farfrae's house. He then tells her that he plans to leave Casterbridge. She tries to persuade him not to go. She says that she may soon marry Mr. Farfrae and that she would like him to be present at her wedding.

She confesses that she hadn't told him of her love for Farfrae because she feared he would not approve.

Henchard is moved by her confession but cannot change his mind. He gives his approval for anything she wants to do. He refuses to stay for her wedding, but asks that she think of him kindly in future. Henchard dresses again as a laborer and leaves town.

Elizabeth-Jane meets Newson at Farfrae's house. She is shocked to discover that Henchard lied to her father about her death. In spite of her promise to think kindly of Henchard, she feels that she cannot.

## Commentary

The chapter focusses on Henchard and his emotional suffering. His fear that Newson might return is finally fulfilled when Newson returns to claim his daughter. Henchard's affection for Elizabeth-Jane is so great that he cannot bear the prospect of her reproach when she discovers his lie. He therefore decides to leave Casterbridge rather than to endure Elizabeth-Jane's anger.

Newson dismisses Henchard's act as insignificant, but Elizabeth-Jane is shocked at her stepfather's deception.

The pathos of Henchard's parting from Elizabeth-Jane wins sympathy for him.

*éclat*: (French) distinction, brilliance.
*via*: (Latin) road, way.
*schiedam*: (Dutch) gin.
**Cain:** in the Biblical story, Cain lamented that his punishment was more than he could bear.

QUESTION: How is Henchard's leaving town dressed as a hay trusser linked with his coming to the town years before?

## CHAPTER 44

### Summary

Henchard walks for five days, sleeping outside because parting from Elizabeth-Jane has so distressed him that he cannot meet other people. He travels to Weydon-Priors, where the fair had been held 25 years before, when he parted from Susan and his daughter. He carries mementos of Elizabeth-Jane in his pack, and finds that he is unable to go far from Casterbridge and her. Thus, he travels from place to place in a circle around Casterbridge.

He finds work at his old job as a hay trusser. As he works, he thinks of how many people die every day who long to live, and how he longs to die but lives on. He listens for news of Casterbridge and the wedding. When he learns the day, he sets out to see Elizabeth-Jane and ask her forgiveness. He buys a goldfinch in a cage to give to her as a wedding present. His decision to go to Casterbridge is made "by a sudden reckless determination." He resolves to overcome his pride and ask for pardon from Elizabeth-Jane.

Henchard arrives in Casterbridge on Elizabeth-Jane's wedding day but avoids the wedding festivities. He asks in the kitchen to see Mrs. Farfrae. The servant takes him to a little room to wait, and Elizabeth-Jane comes to him from the dancing. When she sees who it is, she stops smiling and calls him "Mr. Henchard." Henchard appeals to her not to be so cold, but she reminds him of his lie to her father. He feels so overwhelmed that he cannot defend himself. He leaves her, asking forgiveness and assuring her that he will never trouble her again.

## Commentary

The pathos of this chapter is greater than any before. Henchard has endured suffering before, but he is now completely isolated and without hope. His decision to return to Casterbridge to see Elizabeth-Jane is an attempt to overcome his pride and to acknowledge the importance of love. His effort fails because he is unable to speak when Elizabeth-Jane accuses him. He has come to value himself so little that he cannot speak in his own defence. His wedding gift is forgotten, as the purpose of the visit fails.

The quickness of Henchard's departure, "before [Elizabeth-Jane] could collect her thoughts," is appropriate to his impulsive nature. His abruptness and the shame that prevents him from explaining his action deny him the forgiveness he has sought.

**quickset:** a hawthorn hedge.
*pari passu:* (Latin) with equal step, at the same time.
**St. Martin's Day:** November 11.
**Samson:** the Biblical character whose strength was lost when Delilah cut his hair.

QUESTION: What is the importance of Henchard's decision to return to Casterbridge to ask Elizabeth-Jane's forgiveness?

# CHAPTER 45

## Summary

One week after the wedding, Elizabeth-Jane discovers the birdcage with the goldfinch dead in it near the house. Three weeks after that, she learns from the servants that Henchard had been seen carrying the cage. She realizes that it was intended as a wedding present and a gesture of apology, and her heart softens. She and Farfrae are alone, as Newson has moved to a house near the sea. They begin to search for Henchard.

They take the road to Weatherby and are just about to turn back when they meet Abel Whittle. He tells them that Henchard has just died in a cottage nearby.

Whittle tells how he followed Henchard when he left Casterbridge after seeing Elizabeth-Jane. He persisted, although Henchard repeatedly told him to return to the town. Whittle found an empty cottage to house his old employer when he became too ill to walk. He tended Henchard in his illness, in gratitude for Henchard's kindness to his mother when she was alive.

Elizabeth-Jane and Farfrae go to the cottage and read Henchard's will. It asks that no one tell Elizabeth-Jane of his death, that no proper burial be arranged, and that no one remember or mourn him. The despair of his last moments is clear in his will, and Elizabeth-Jane weeps at the memory of the unkindness of her parting with her stepfather. She follows the instructions of Henchard's will as far as possible.

Elizabeth-Jane and Farfrae live on happily, but Elizabeth-Jane has been taught by her experience the inescapable nature of pain.

## Commentary

Henchard becomes a tragic figure. His solitary death and the despair expressed in his will are, as Elizabeth-Jane recognizes, "a piece of the same stuff that his whole life was made of." But the will suggests changes, too. Henchard acts to protect Elizabeth-Jane from sorrow.

Abel Whittle's loyalty to his former employer shows the importance of kindness and generous actions, such as Henchard's to Whittle's mother. This is parallelled when Henchard tries to be kind to his stepdaughter.

Elizabeth-Jane's discovery of the starved goldfinch is an appropriate beginning to her search for her stepfather, because Henchard is starved for love and forgiveness. Henchard's physical illness, in which he cannot take food, is a reflection of his spiritual state, in which he is cut off from love and affection and hope. His death is tragic, but his strength in bearing suffering is admirable. He is mourned by Elizabeth-Jane and, thus, wins the forgiveness and the affection he had sought.

**antipodean:** the other side of the world. The reference is to criminal sentences of exile to Australia.
**assize town:** the town where civil and criminal cases are tried.
**Minerva:** goddess of wisdom.
**Diana Multimammia:** many-breasted Diana. The burial mounds look like breasts.
**wambled:** staggered.
**Capharaum:** Biblical place of darkness.

QUESTION: What is the significance of each term of Henchard's will?

# Character Sketches

## Michael Henchard

Henchard is a strong man, energetic, impulsive and hard-working. He is honest and just, but also rash and impetuous. Thus, although he sincerely works to make amends to Susan for his impulsive action, he continues to be impulsive in his treatment of other people. To make the fight fair, he binds one arm when he fights Farfrae. He also refuses to keep any part of his property from his creditors when he goes bankrupt. He is scrupulous in his honesty and in his consideration for other people's financial needs. He is generous to Lucetta, to Abel Whittle's mother, to Susan and to Farfrae.

Opposed to this generous side of Henchard's nature is a darker side. He punishes Abel Whittle for his lateness with such harshness that Farfrae accuses him of tyranny. He is affectionate with Farfrae, but also is overbearing and demanding. He becomes Farfrae's enemy because of pride and jealousy. He fails to confess the past to Elizabeth-Jane because of pride. He cannot tell her why he lied to Newson because he is afraid to reveal his affection for her and his fear of losing her affection.

In spite of the flaws in his character, Henchard has great strength. This strength is apparent in his ability to endure suffering for his actions. His 21-year oath of abstinence is a sign of strength of will. He endures his fall from prosperity because of the strength of his character.

Henchard completely despairs only after it seems impossible to make any reparation to Elizabeth-Jane for his lie to her father. The terms of his will are a defiant renunciation of any connection with other human beings, and yet his last act is an attempt to win forgiveness from Elizabeth-Jane for his selfish act.

Henchard's character is convincing because of the contradictions in his nature. He dominates the novel and achieves a greatness of stature in spite of his failures.

## Susan Henchard (Newson)

Susan is meek, self-sacrificing and affectionate. She accepts Henchard's outrageous action in selling her because she has borne his bad temper as long as she can. She goes with Newson because he seems kind and is willing to take responsibility for her and Elizabeth-Jane. Her sense of justice is shown by her recognition that Henchard's action frees her from her obligations to him.

Susan remains loyal to Newson until a friend questions the legality of her situation. She keeps her first marriage a secret from her daughter. Like Henchard, she is proud and fears that the shame of the past will destroy Elizabeth-Jane's love for her.

Susan is pessimistic. Although she actively seeks her first husband again, to save Elizabeth-Jane from poverty, she is not hopeful about the future. Her death is not a surprise because her marriage to Newson, which seems to have been happy, is over and she has saved Elizabeth-Jane from poverty.

### Elizabeth-Jane Newson

Elizabeth-Jane is taught by poverty and by the loss of her father to endure hardship. She, like her mother, is pessimistic, but she is also responsive to beauty and to love. She devotes herself to study and has great instinctive understanding and sensitivity. She loves Farfrae, and comes to love Henchard as she loved Susan. Although she renounces Henchard for lying to her about her father, she regrets her harshness and searches for her lost stepfather. Elizabeth-Jane shows no jealousy when Farfrae courts Lucetta. She is modest and unassuming. She is affectionate and responsive to Farfrae's courtship. Although she feels the burden of human suffering, she also feels the joys of life. She does not forget either.

### Donald Farfrae

Farfrae is a young Scotsman, whose charm and intelligence make him popular. He is mechanically adept and a good businessman. He is able to express emotion in song and to be pleasant company. Unlike Henchard, Farfrae is not rash in his dealing with others, except in the case of his love affair with Lucetta. His prudent attitudes and his affection for Henchard, which persist in spite of Henchard's anger, suggest the harmony of his nature with Elizabeth-Jane's rather than with Lucetta's. His marriage to Elizabeth-Jane confirms this harmony.

### Lucetta Templeman (Le Sueur)

Lucetta is of French descent and inherits money after living in poverty. She uses her money to buy clothes. Her attention to clothes is a contrast to Elizabeth-Jane's decision not to dress showily. Lucetta is indiscreet in her association with Henchard in Jersey and in her letters to him about their relationship. She is unstable in her affections, as she falls in love with Farfrae while she is waiting to marry Henchard. She deceives Henchard, by her secret marriage, and Farfrae, by not telling him her past. She dies when she knows that he must learn what she has done.

### Richard Newson

Newson is a kind and jovial man. He takes pity on Susan when Henchard taunts and shames her at the fair. He is a loving father to Elizabeth-Jane and so considerate as a husband that he leaves his daughter and wife when Susan fears that their union is not legal. He is a trusting man and takes Henchard's word that Elizabeth-Jane is dead. He forgives Henchard's lie when he returns and finds his daughter.

# Literary Elements

## Plot and Structure

*The Mayor of Casterbridge* is unified by its emphasis on Michael Henchard. The novel is structured as a tragedy, presenting the rise and fall of Henchard's fortunes. To make Henchard's fall credible, Hardy uses the first two chapters of the novel to describe the rash action that, after almost 20 years, directly affects Henchard's life. The prologue establishes Henchard's character and the past from which Susan and Elizabeth-Jane, Newson and the furmity woman later emerge.

To emphasize the importance of past actions, Hardy uses many parallels and repetitions. Thus, Susan and Elizabeth-Jane return to the fair at Weydon-Priors along the same road that Henchard travelled with Susan and their daughter at the beginning of the novel. Henchard returns alone to Weydon-Priors, 25 years after his first arrival there, dressed again as a hay trusser. The repetition emphasizes his return to the state in which he first entered the town.

Another repetition occurs when Henchard meets first Susan and then Lucetta at the Ring. The ruined and gloomy setting is an appropriate reflection in each case of the characters' states of mind.

Hardy describes Farfrae's career as parallel to Henchard's, although moving in opposite directions. The young Scotsman arrives in Casterbridge, as Henchard had, with nothing. Like Henchard, he becomes prosperous and is honored by the position of mayor. He even marries Lucetta, the woman who had promised to marry Henchard. His rise to prosperity echoes Henchard's and takes place at the same time as Henchard's fall. Henchard buys grain in great quantity, then sells at a loss. Then Farfrae buys up the grain at a low price, and makes a profit when the price soars after bad weather at harvest time. The two men, who have been friends and who have worked together, are separated ever further by the divergence of their fortunes as Farfrae rises and Henchard falls.

The influence of the past is important. Accordingly, Susan reappears in Henchard's life, Newson returns and the furmity woman arrives in Casterbridge.

Elizabeth-Jane's return is significantly different from the other returns. Henchard assumes that she is Elizabeth-Jane, his daughter. She is actually Susan's daughter by the sailor, Newson.

Henchard's rejection of Elizabeth-Jane when he discovers her parternity is important. By this act, he not only becomes lonely and unhappy, but he rejects responsibility for what happened to Susan. He had accepted this responsibility when he took his oath of abstinence and when he remarried Susan.

After Lucetta's death, Henchard comes to feel affection for Elizabeth-Jane, but acts to protect that affection by lying to her real father. When he returns to Casterbridge on Elizabeth-Jane's wedding day, Henchard is deeply repentant. He is able to see that affection is more important than pride, to accept the past completely and to understand the scope of his responsibility.

Coincidence plays a role in the action when the sailor happens by the tent where Henchard is trying to sell his wife and when the furmity woman happens to come to Casterbridge 20 years later. The coincidences serve to reinforce Hardy's view that "Character is Fate," events happen because of what the characters do. Thus, although the furmity woman's appearance in court when Henchard is judge is a coincidence, the effect of her arrival — the revelation of Henchard's shameful past — is inevitable. Similarly, Newson's returns are coincidental, but serve to reveal facts that cannot be hidden permanently.

Hardy uses coincidence to suggest the powerlessness of the individual and, at the same time, to insist on the primary importance of character. The action of the novel is determined by Henchard's actions in the past and in the present. Although he feels that he is the victim of fate, he is the victim only of his own character. Hardy uses the structure of the novel to unite action and character.

# Theme

In *The Mayor of Casterbridge*, Hardy emphasizes man's responsibility for his actions. Henchard cannot escape the past and must acknowledge that he is responsible for his fate. He suffers and his actions cause others to suffer.

He learns to accept his responsibility for such suffering first by keeping for 21 years the oath of abstinence, which serves as a constant reminder of his shameful act. Then he remarries Susan to make amends to her. His hardest lesson to learn is that he must also accept the past over which he had no direct control: he must learn to love Elizabeth-Jane for herself, although she is Newson's daughter and not his own.

Henchard lies to Newson about Elizabeth-Jane's death

because of the love he feels for her and because he fears losing her love. He decides to leave Casterbridge rather than endure the anger and scorn that Elizabeth-Jane will feel when she discovers what he has done. He returns to Casterbridge only to beg forgiveness, having learned the importance of love and the need to accept the responsibility for his actions. His love for Elizabeth-Jane, whose birth was the result of his treatment of Susan, is the positive counterpart to the despair expressed in his will.

Hardy's portrait of Michael Henchard may be seen as pessimistic, for Henchard suffers and dies alone. Henchard's strength and his ability to grow and to feel love contradict this pessimism, however. Henchard is a tragic figure who inspires not only pity but admiration. "Character is Fate," and Henchard accepts the consequences of his nature or fate.

## Setting

Like Hardy's other major novels, *The Mayor of Casterbridge* is set in Wessex. The countryside, with its towns and villages, provides a realistic background. Henchard's wandering at the end of the novel and Newson's journey to Casterbridge and return to the seaside are concretely located in a specific region.

Hardy describes the town of Casterbridge in detail. The busy marketplace, overlooked by High-Place Hall, and Henchard's house with its offices and granary attached are vividly described. The town's three inns, the King's Arms, the Three Mariners, and Peter's Finger, represent the three levels of Casterbridge society. The official function at which Henchard presides as mayor takes place at the King's Arms. The townspeople make merry and delight in Farfrae's singing at the Three Mariners, where Elizabeth-Jane and Susan also stay, and Elizabeth-Jane helps with the serving. Peter's Finger is a thoroughly disreputable inn where the poorest townspeople drink and plan the skimmity ride. It serves as a refuge for poachers and other minor criminals. Hardy describes each of the inns in detail to suggest the degeneration of Henchard's status as he moves from the position of prominence in the King's Arms to become a tool in the hands of the guests at Peter's Finger, when they read his letters from Lucetta and plan the skimmity ride.

The Roman ruins and other remnants from the past, such as the ruined priory, serve as a witness to the enduring presence of history. The past haunts Henchard, and survives in physical landmarks. Hardy frequently uses these ruins and remains as background for the action of the novel.

The most important function of setting is its reflection or expression of the characters' moods. Henchard, in his despair, walks beside the ruined priory where a gallows stands. When he feels complete desperation, he walks beside the river in the dark. Lucetta meets Henchard at twilight at the Ring, and the place, with its gloomy associations, reflects her fears that Henchard will reveal her past to Farfrae and destroy her happiness.

Hardy also uses setting as a counterpoint to the characters' moods. Thus, when Henchard looks outside the tent after he has sold his wife, he sees the serene and peaceful landscape made rosy by the last rays of the setting sun. Hardy directly contrasts the noisy, cruel and destructive scene inside the tent with the grandeur, beauty and calm of the natural setting.

He uses contrast in another way when Henchard and Susan meet in the Ring. The gloom of the place and its associations of cruelty seem inappropriate to their reunion and plans for the future. The setting *is* appropriate, however, to the problems Henchard encounters in the future. The setting thus gives a forecast of what Henchard must endure.

## Style

Hardy's narrative style is that of the ominiscient narrator. This gives him a point of view that allows him to comment upon the action, to place himself in the mind of a character to give us reasons and motives, and to philosophize or describe the background to clarify whatever point he wishes to make.

Hardy's writing is usually clear. If a long descriptive passage seems to interrupt the action, we should remember Hardy's uses for the natural setting.

The opening pages of the novel display Hardy's ability to write prose that delineated character, background and circumstances from an omniscient narrator's point of view. The excellent description, especially of Susan's face and of the young couple's manner of walking, reveals that they are unhappily married, that the man is discontented and that Susan is pessimistic. Furthermore, the dry dust, the barren countryside and the "blackened-green stage of colour" of the vegetation lend an oppressive air to the scene as a prelude to the dark events to come. Hardy reveals his mastery of setting, mood and character throughout the novel.

His ability in writing dialogue is evident on two levels. The dialogue reflects his characters' social position while it adds to our knowledge of their personalities. A passage from Chapter 9 illustrates this. Henchard makes a final appeal to Farfrae:

> Now I am not the man to let a cause be lost for want of a word. And before ye are gone for ever I'll speak. Once more, will ye stay? There it is, flat and plain. You can see that it isn't all selfishness that makes me press 'ee; for my business is not quite so scientific as to require an intellect entirely out of the common. Others would do for the place without doubt. Some selfishness perhaps there is, but there is more; it isn't for me to repeat what. Come bide with me — and name your own terms. I'll agree to 'em willingly and 'ithout a word gainsaying; for, hang it, Farfrae, I like thee well.

This example shows Henchard's blunt character. Not a word is wasted, and he comes directly to the point. He uses rural expressions, but does not speak like the lower-class townspeople. Furthermore, his impetuous nature is shown by his concerted attempt to hire Farfrae because he likes him and to press his immediate friendship, without the normal preliminaries, by insisting that Farfrae come to breakfast.

Farfrae's kind and fair disposition is brought out by his speeches. His reasonableness and sweetness contrast with Henchard's struggles. His unwillingness to commit an act of vengeance or meanness, and his Scottish economy of speech are apparent in these passages from Chapter 34:

> About that little seedsman's shop, . . . the shop overlooking the churchyard, which is to let. It is not for myself I want it, but for our unlucky fellow-townsman Henchard. It would be a new beginning for him, if a small one; and I have told the Council that I would head a private subscription among them to set him up in it — that I would be fifty pounds, if they would make up other fifty among them.

> But I cannot discharge a man who was once a good friend to me. How can I forget that when I came here 'twas he enabled me to make a footing for myself? No, no. As long as I've a day's wark to offer he shall do it if

he chooses. 'Tis not I who will deny him such a little as
that. But I'll drop the idea of establishing him in a shop
till I can think more about it.

Lucetta's letters reveal her character, as do most of her
speeches. Her candor shows an element of abandon that Hardy
links to her French background. The letters and her bantering
with Farfrae show a certain sophisticated ability to play with
words in a teasing way. Her frivolous nature is revealed by her
flirting and teasing.

Through her speech, Hardy shows the gradual change that
takes place in Elizabeth-Jane. She turns more and more to study
and reflection. At the end of the novel, the reader finds
Elizabeth-Jane a melancholy but kind and affectionate woman.

Hardy's use of dialect in the speech of the townspeople and
in Elizabeth-Jane's and Henchard's conversation gives color to
the dialogue in the novel. Farfrae's Scottish speech adds diversi-
ty. Dialect also serves a social function, for Henchard ridicules
Elizabeth-Jane's dialect as inappropriate to her social position.

Atmosphere is an important aspect of Hardy's style. He uses
the events of the novel to comment on man's situation, and the
recurrent moments of loss, separation and suffering contribute
to the gloom of the picture. His characters refer to fate and prov-
idence, but Hardy is able to suggest at the same time the importance of the characters' own actions. Thus, the pessimism and
darkness of the novel are balanced by a sense of the characters'
strength. Henchard endures terrible suffering but learns the importance of love. Elizabeth-Jane endures great sorrow but finds
happiness with Farfrae. Hardy presents both tragedy and hope.

Hardy achieves realism by details of description, by the use
of dialect in the conversation of the townspeople, by the introduction of facts about the period of transition in agriculture
and its effect on rural England in the mid-nineteenth century, and
by providing psychologically convincing portraits of his
characters. He uses realism to ground the novel in fact and to give
susbtance to the tragedy of his story. Henchard is a convincing
human being, described in the real world of the grain business
and of domestic affairs. He achieves the stature of a tragic figure,
but remains sympathetic and understandable because of the
realism of Hardy's picture of his everyday life.

This combination of tragedy and homely realism is the
hallmark of Hardy's style.

# Irony

Irony is created when there is a discrepancy between what is expected and what happens, between what is apparently true and what is in fact true. Irony plays an important role in *The Mayor of Casterbridge*. Henchard's relationship with Farfrae is one of the major ironies. Henchard pleads with Farfrae to stay in Casterbridge; he confesses his past to the young man and makes him a partner in his business. Then, Farfrae supplants Henchard as a successful grain merchant and as owner of Henchard's house. He becomes the husband of the woman who had planned to marry Henchard, and mayor of the town.

Similarly, when Henchard decides to tell Elizabeth-Jane that he is her father, he discovers, while looking for documentary proof, Susan's letter with its revelation that Elizabeth-Jane is Newson's daughter. Henchard expected to find comfort in revealing the truth of his relationship to Elizabeth-Jane, but found instead the pain of another deception.

Hardy uses irony to emphasize the limitations of human understanding. He suggests that the outcome of any action is unexpected.

# Suspense

Hardy uses suspense when he describes Henchard's involvement with Lucetta immediately after Henchard and Susan have reunited and plan to remarry. The story suggests possible complications. Henchard himself wonders if making amends will be as easy as it seems.

The suspense is sometimes more dramatic, as when Lucetta jumps out from behind the curtains, expecting to see Henchard, and sees a stranger. By ending the chapter with this surprise, Hardy arouses our curiosity about the identity of the unknown man.

At the end of another chapter, when Jopp tells Henchard that a sea captain has been asking for him, we are left to wonder about his identity until the sailor arrives the next day and reveals himself as Newson, Susan's second husband.

Hardy uses suspense in a more general way as he builds up a sense of the pervasive power of the past.

# Names

Although Hardy does not, like Dickens, use names as indicators of character, he chooses suggestive names. Thus, Farfrae's name indicates that he is *frae*, free. Henchard's name derives from the Middle English word, *hengestman* or groom, suggesting that he is a servant who must follow his master. Abel Whittle's name suggests his link with Henchard, who identifies himself with Cain. The weather prophet's name, Mr. Fall, may suggest what will follow Henchard's trust in him. These are simply suggestions, however. Hardy is more concerned with realistic characterization than with the simplistic identification of character through names.

## Symbolism

The goldfinch that Henchard brings to Elizabeth-Jane as a wedding present is forgotten and left to starve in his cage. The bird becomes a symbol of Henchard himself, for he is starved for affection and dies. Elizabeth-Jane is moved to search for her stepfather by the sight of the bird and by the knowledge of Henchard's desire for a reconciliation.

The bad wheat, which is responsible for the bad bread the townspeople complain of when Susan and Elizabeth-Jane first come to Casterbridge, is another symbol. Henchard disclaims responsibility for the problem, saying that he was taken in by the wheat. He is eager to save the situation, however, and advertises for a manager to help him avoid such problems in future. He is similarly eager to remedy the suffering he has caused for Susan and Elizabeth-Jane. The bad wheat thus stands as a symbol of the past that Henchard hopes to redeem.

## Animal Imagery

Hardy uses animal imagery to comment on his characters and their actions. After Henchard has sold Susan, for example, Hardy describes the horses outside the tent. They are harnessed and, thus, in servitude, but they are "rubbing each other lovingly" in spite of their servitude. Their acceptance of their lot and the affection they show contrast with Henchard's rejection of his responsibilities and his cruel treatment of Susan.

Later in the novel, the episode in which the bull chases Lucetta and Elizabeth-Jane shows the ferocity of the animal world. The violence of the incident has no destructive effect, however. The contrast is made between this apparently dangerous situation and the skimmity ride, by which the townspeople intend only to shame Lucetta. Their performance in fact causes her death.

Henchard saves Lucetta and Elizabeth-Jane from the bull.

He is as strong as a bull. He also behaves like a bull breaking out of his pen when he interrupts the ceremony planned for the royal visitor. His actions are not murderous and he is "mastered" by Elizabeth-Jane's affection.

Hardy uses references to animals for contrast and parallel to his characters' actions. He introduces the caged goldfinch as a symbol of Henchard himself. The bird starves to death and Henchard dies, starved of the affection he sought. The direct relationship between Henchard and the bird is suggested when Elizabeth-Jane finds the dead bird and immediately sets off to search for her stepfather.

## Dialect

Hardy uses dialect words and phrases that he learned from listening to country people in his native region, the southwest of England. The Casterbridge townspeople talk in dialect to increase the realism of the novel and to add local color.

The use of dialect also identifies a social class that Henchard, as mayor and a prosperous merchant, has risen above. Although he occasionally speaks in dialect, he criticizes Elizabeth-Jane when she uses a "country phrase." His criticism is an expression of his anger that she is not his own daughter, but he uses her improper speech as an excuse for that anger.

In his preface, Hardy defends the Scottish dialect of Farfrae's conversation as an accurate representation of Scottish speech. Farfrae's manner of speaking adds variety to the dialogue in the novel and helps to characterize him.

## Allusion

By brief reference to an incident or character known to the reader, a writer can suggest a contrast or parallel to an action or character. Hardy refers to Biblical characters, mythological figures and to literary events and characters. Henchard is compared to Cain and to Bellerophon; the allusions describe his guilt and his punishment of loneliness and suffering.

Allusion may be direct, as the references to Cain and Bellerophoan are, or it may be ironic. The allusion to Calpurnia, Julius Caesar's loyal wife, to describe Lucetta is ironic because Lucetta's loyalty is called into question by her past. Her failure to keep her promise to Henchard separates her from the faithfulness represented by Calpurnia.

# Description

Hardy's descriptions of Casterbridge, High-Place Hall, the Ring and the ruined priory are vivid pictorial representations. He uses physical details and direct comments about each spot to give a realistic picture of the novel's settings. His architectural knowledge helps him to describe buildings accurately.

# Melodrama

The wife auction with which the novel begins may seem melodramatic, but, as Hardy points out in the preface, such an event did happen "in the real history of the town called Casterbridge and the neighbouring country."

The reading of Lucetta's love letters to Henchard seems hard to believe, but Lucetta's lack of discretion makes the exposure of her past credible. The fight between Henchard and Farfrae is another instance of melodrama, but it is linked to Henchard's character and appropriate to his other actions.

Hardy uses melodramatic incidents with success because he firmly links those incidents to the characteristics of the people involved. Thus, the furmity woman's appearance after 20 years is convincing because Henchard himself seems ready for the revelation of his past and for the burden of shame.

# Tragedy

Hardy structures *The Mayor of Casterbridge* as a tragedy. Henchard achieves the stature of a tragic hero through the weight of suffering that he bears, brought on by his own actions. Like King Lear, his downfall begins with a rash act. Selling Susan is like Lear's rejection of Cordelia. Although Hardy's novel does not reach the poetic heights of Shakespeare's play, it does pose serious questions about the nature of human life through the portrait of Michael Henchard, his suffering and the suffering that others endure because of him.

# Contrast

The contrasting personalities of Henchard and Farfrae are at the center of the novel. Lucetta and Elizabeth-Jane are also opposite natures, and Lucetta's search for Henchard contrasts with Susan's search.

Lucetta's rejection of the past shows her shallowness and contrasts with what Henchard learns. The parallel between them, as they both lie about the past, emphasizes the difference between Lucetta's hysteria and fear, and Henchard's final acceptance of the burden he has created for himself.

Hardy uses contrasts to pattern the events in the novel.

# Selected Criticisms

Hardy has been called by Virginia Woolf, "the greatest tragic writer among English novelists." He has been praised for the realism of his characterization and for his creation of individuals who reveal the complexity of human life. He has been described as a philosopher because his novels deal with ideas about the human situation. The selections below suggest the range of critical response to *The Mayor of Casterbridge*.

That Hardy's was a native and persistent order of genius; that he expressed it in a style and drama which he made unmistakably his own; that his work carries the stamp of a theme and vision which have impressed a large area of art and experience . . . that he exists as a force in modern literature in spite of some of the severest critical reservation any notable writer has been subjected to — these we may take as facts . . .

Virginia Woolf, when she visited him at Max Gate in 1926, was sincere in recognizing a fact of history. "I wanted him to say one word about his writings before we left and could only ask which of his books he would have chosen if, like me, he had had to choose one to read in the train. I had taken *The Mayor of Casterbridge* . . . 'And did it hold your interest?' he asked. I stammered that I could not stop reading it, which was true, but sounded wrong." Few readers have missed the spell.

Morton Dauwen Zabel, *Craft and Character
in Modern Fiction*. New York: The Viking Press, Inc. (1940).

The high degree of coincidence in the typical Hardy narrative has been noted by all observers, often unfavorably. Mr. Samuel Chew explains it as partly a result of the influence of the "sensation novelists," and partly as a deliberate emphasis on "the persistence of the unforeseen" . . . The logic of the traditional story is not the logic of modern literary fiction. The traditional story admits, and even cherishes, the improbable and unpredictable. The miraculous, or nearly miraculous, is what makes a story a story, in the old way. Unless a story has some strange and unusual features it will hardly be told and will not be remembered. Most of the anecdotes that Hardy records in his journal savor of the odd and unusual. And occasionally he speaks directly to the point, as in the following passages:

The writer's problem is, how to strike the balance between the uncommon and the ordinary, so as on the one hand to give interest, on the other to give reality.

In working out this problem, human nature must never be abnormal, which is introducing incredibility. The uncommonness must be in the events, not in the characters . . . [July, 1881].

A story must be exceptional enough to justify its telling. We taletellers are all Ancient Mariners, and none of us is warranted in stopping Wedding Guests (in other words, the hurrying public) unless he has something more unusual to relate than the ordinary experience of every average man and woman.

Thus coincidence in Hardy's narratives represents a conviction about the nature of story as such.

Donald Davidson, *Still Rebels, Still Yankees, and Other Essays*. Baton Rouge: The Louisiana State Press, (1957)

The traditional basis of *The Mayor of Casterbridge* as tragedy emerges at once in the . . . hyperbolical quality of its first episode. Discouraged by his failure to get on in the world and impatient of ordinary domestic restraints, Michael Henchard . . . in a drunken moment sells his wife to a sailor for five guineas. Clearly calculated to startle the imagination, to appeal to its sense for the grand and the heroic in human experience, Henchard's act of violence bears the same relation to the novel as the betrayal of Cordelia and the murder of Laius to *Lear* and *Oedipus*.

John Paterson, "*The Mayor of Casterbridge* as Tragedy." *Victorian Studies* 3 (1959)

It may be said of Thomas Hardy (who at times seemed the kind of man to whom nothing happens) that he blundered and stumbled onto greatness . . . One of his humble ambitions, until fairly late in his novelistic career, was to be considered a "good hand at a serial"; he gave little thought to fiction as an art. And though he always cherished poetry as a fine uncompromising art, he waited many years before publishing a volume of verse. He even seemed, at times, a passive spectator of his own career and life. And yet this apparently shy, reticent, unassuming, even unambitious man achieved almost equal eminence as novelist and poet, and died the Grand Old Man of English letters. A subversive writer without intending to be one, he was honored at the end by the Establishment, with burial in Westminster Abbey and the Prime Minister as a pallbearer . . . He had begun his career as a novelist in the days of Dickens and Trollope, yet published a large volume of verse three years after *The Waste Land* and a year before *The Sun Also Rises*.

Albert J. Guerard, Introduction to
*Hardy: A Collection of Critical Essays*,
Englewood Cliffs, N.J.: Prentice-Hall, (1963).

*The Mayor of Casterbridge* is, in construction and force, Hardy's finest novel. It is certainly the most artistic of the major novels, if artistry may be taken to mean the resistance to the easy way of doing things, resistance to the kind of writing that makes for popular serials. Hardy does not allow himself the dubious luxury of descriptive set pieces, quaint characters, or complex plotting in this novel nearly so much as he was inclined to do in other works, even great ones. His focus on a single main character with other characters subordinately grouped around him shows fewer marks of the architect's drawing board than do most of the other novels, and provides a trenchant unity. The tracing of Henchard's descent into the lower depths, derived as it is with remorseless logic from his character and probabilities of event associated with it, is the essence of grand tragedy. Finally, the very creation of a character like Henchard is an accomplishment of the highest sort. He belongs with Oedipus and Ahab, with Lord Jim and Othello.

Richard C. Carpenter, *Thomas Hardy*.
New York: Twayne Publishers, Inc. (1964).

In *The Mayor of Casterbridge* the town is . . . an enclosed community in which the focus of the novel is the rivalry in commerce and the love of the two mayors, Henchard and Farfrae . . . In Henchard, stubborn and unreasoning as he is, Hardy creates the first truly dominant individual in his novels . . . 'Part of his wish to wash his hands of life arose from his perception of its contrarious inconsistencies' (ch.44); and in that one sentence is contained the first direct statement of an understanding that life is inconsistent, because it involves two such contrary features as the

76

logic of nature's laws and the illogicality of human emotions. Elizabeth-Jane . . . is the first to ask 'What that chaos called consciousness, which spun in her . . . like a top, tended to, and began in' (ch.18). But she, like Farfrae, is ready to bend with the vicissitudes of life . . . It is Henchard who shakes his fist at the universe . . . There is an overwhelming feeling of despair in his understanding of life . . .

Andrew Enstice, "The Fruit of the Tree
of Knowledge," in *The Novels of Thomas Hardy*.
London: Vision Press (1979).

Henchard's disaster is bound up very specifically with his wife, his child, and his lover . . .

The first Elizabeth-Jane . . . was the symbol, living and visible, of the early married life of Henchard and Susan . . . and whatever there was between them dies with her.

Rosalind Miles, "The Women of Wessex,"
in *The Novels of Thomas Hardy*.
London: Vision Press (1979).

The complexity of the web of relationships between the six major characters in *The Mayor of Casterbridge* is partly brought about and greatly augmented by the truly remarkable amount of lying which is done. Henchard pretends to have a sufficiently respectable past for him to be Mayor of Casterbridge, which involves him in the particular pretences of being a widower and of courting Susan on her return. He pretends not to have known Lucetta before she came to Casterbridge, which involves another pretended courtship (or attempt at it). He pretends to Elizabeth-Jane that she is his daughter, which involves him in the further pretences to her that Newson is dead and to Newson that Elizabeth-Jane is dead. Susan pretends to Elizabeth-Jane that Henchard is barely more than an acquaintance and to Henchard that Elizabeth-Jane is his daughter. Newson pretends to Susan that their 'marriage' is valid, and when that pretence fails he pretends to be dead. Lucetta, over whose door in Casterbridge is the image of a mask which has now been almost chipped away, pretends not to have known Henchard before she came to Casterbridge and, for a time, pretends not to know Farfrae. All speak 'mad lies like a child, in pure mockery of consequences,' as is said of Henchard when he sends Newson away from Casterbridge grieving.

Every single one of these lies is a lie about a relationship and represents in part an attempt to conform to orthodox rules about relationships. The necessity for each lie arises because the rules have been transgressed (only Farfrae and Elizabeth-Jane, the two thoroughly successful innocents, transgress but fail to see the need for lying). The relationships lied about are all affected by the preordained obligations of marriage and parenthood, of which ground rules common to both are that the relationships should be exclusive and irreversible . . .

The collapse of each of these lies compels change. When the selling of Susan is told in court, Henchard's relationship with the whole world changes. When his connection with Lucetta is known, Lucetta dies (thus escaping the impossibility, according to the rules, of living in the same town with two 'husbands'). In anticipation of Elizabeth-Jane's learning . . . that Henchard is not her father and that Newson her real father is alive, Henchard leaves the town and solves the problem of Elizabeth-Jane's two fathers. Henchard's discovery of Elizabeth-Jane's real origins makes him look on her as an intrusive stranger, not as a daughter . . .

Henchard . . . is finally driven to learn that relationships don't reside in law or blood.

Juliet M. Grindle, "Compulsion and Choice
in *The Mayor of Casterbridge*,"
in *The Novels of Thomas Hardy*.
London: Vision Press (1979).

# Review Questions and Answers

## Question 1.
How does irony figure in *The Mayor of Casterbridge*?

**Answer**

This novel can be regarded as a series of ironies. The major irony in the novel concerns Henchard's relationship with Farfrae. Henchard implores Farfrae to stay in Casterbridge. It is this same Farfrae who stays to capture Henchard's business, Henchard's lover, Henchard's daughter and even Henchard's position as mayor. Similarly, just as Henchard begins to love Elizabeth-Jane, he discovers that she is another man's daughter. Farfrae comes to Lucetta's house to court Elizabeth-Jane but remains to marry Lucetta. Henchard does Lucetta a great favor when he agrees to return her letters, but this act destroys Lucetta by providing material for the skimmity ride.

There are innumerable other ironies. In the scene in which Susan questions the furmity woman, Elizabeth-Jane questions the propriety of talking to such a woman. "Don't speak to her — it isn't respectable," she tells her mother, not realizing how disreputable her mother's own past is. This sort of irony appears repeatedly throughout the novel. The characters are constantly involved in situations for which they are ill equipped, since they must rely on deceptions and half-truths.

Hardy uses irony to suggest the inadequacy of man's understanding and to emphasize how unexpected the future is.

## Question 2.
How does deception operate in *The Mayor of Casterbridge*?

**Answer**

Deception plays a major role in both plot and theme in *The Mayor of Casterbridge*. Michael Henchard disguises his past. He pretends to be Elizabeth-Jane's father, even after he learns that he is not. Elizabeth-Jane, although not Henchard's daughter, believes that she is. Susan encourages this deception on both sides. Lucetta lies to Farfrae about her past. She comes to Casterbridge to be Henchard's bride, but marries Farfrae. Henchard lies to Lucetta about his former life with Susan. Farfrae comes to Lucetta's home to court Elizabeth-Jane, but marries Lucetta. Even Susan's initial appearance in Casterbridge comes about because a friend has told her she can no longer assume that she is Newson's wife, but must return to her legitimate place with Henchard.

In *The Mayor of Casterbridge*, the deceptions are basic ones involving all of the major areas of life — paternity, love, honor and reputation. They involve fundamental identity. The major characters are involved in a world where relationships and identities are constantly shifting. This confusion about identity focusses the reader's attention on questions about the very basis and nature of human identity.

## Question 3.
What is the function of the townspeople in *The Mayor of Casterbridge*?

## Answer
The townspeople of Casterbridge serve as a chorus to the tragedy unfolding before them. They provide a perspective on the main action. Thus, the reader gets a view of the action through the eyes of the characters involved in that action and still another view of the action through the eyes of the townspeople. Thus the reader is constantly reminded that Henchard is not simply an ordinary man engaged in ordinary activities. From the first, the villagers stress those qualities in Henchard that set him apart from plain people such as them. Henchard as mayor is a large and awesome figure to the townspeople. Similarly, the comments of the villagers indicate Farfrae's charm and, in the skimmity ride, Lucetta's immorality.

Since social aspirations play such a major role in the novel, it is important that the social structure of Casterbridge be clearly delineated. The townspeople are clearly lower class. Their attitudes toward the characters and their actions identify the social demarcations of the town and the position of the characters in this structure. Their comments, for example, about Henchard's marriage to Susan reveal clearly Henchard's accepted position as a leader of the upper class. Their attitude toward Farfrae clearly shows the steps in his reversal of positions with Henchard. The sense of a hierarchy of social position is reinforced through the geographical structure of the town. There are even two bridges, each preserved as the gathering place of a particular social group. Both bridges attract failures, but even the failures are divided into two groups according to their social position. The brick bridge is the gathering place for failures "that did not mind the glare of the public eye." The stone bridge is for the failure "of a politer stamp," who is "sensitive to his own condition." In addition, the townspeople provide comic interludes. They speak in dialect and provide information in the guise of gossip. They add credibility to the events of the novel.

## Question 4.
How does Hardy use symmetrical plotting in *The Mayor of Casterbridge*?

## Answer
The novel balances the downfall of Henchard against the rise of Farfrae. Farfrae's rise in fortune so exactly balances Henchard's destruction that the two men have quite literally exchanged roles. When Henchard first meets Farfrae, the latter is preparing to emigrate to America. Farfrae accepts Henchard's offer of assistance and stays on in Casterbridge. From that point on, the novel chronicles Henchard's loss of power and prosperity and Farfrae's gain of power and prosperity. Each stroke of Henchard's downfall is matched by a rise in Farfrae's fortunes.

Henchard loses money in a grain speculation and finds himself in serious financial difficulty. Simultaneously, Farfrae speculates and finds himself in a good financial situation. Thus, as Henchard withers, Farfrae prospers. Henchard loses Lucetta: Farfrae wins her. Henchard is declared bankrupt, and his name is removed from the sign above the granary, to be replaced by Farfrae's name. In Chapter 32, we find a reversal of earlier roles when Farfrae asks Henchard if he is emigrating and offers his former benefactor assistance. This exchange of roles is completed when Farfrae becomes the mayor of Casterbridge.

Numerous other examples of symmetrical plotting occur throughout the novel. In Chapter 16, for example, Susan is replaced by Lucetta. As Susan dies, a letter from Lucetta arrives. The entire novel is permeated with double situations and events. Henchard has two daughters, Elizabeth-Jane has two fathers, Lucetta has two lovers, Farfrae has two wives, Susan has two husbands.

Similarly, settings are duplicated. The Ring serves as the setting for Henchard's meeting with both Susan and Lucetta, and the road to Weydon-Priors serves as the means of Henchard's arrival and his departure from Casterbridge with his hay-trussing equipment. Newson comes to Casterbridge twice, and Henchard twice meets the old furmity woman. Every important scene in *The Mayor of Casterbridge* seems to be duplicated within the novel.

## Question 5.
How does the statement, "Character is Fate," apply to Henchard?

**Answer**
The novel is dominated by Michael Henchard, and it describes his "Life and Death." He is an impulsive man whose rash action in selling his wife and daughter wins him the freedom he wants but also a burden of guilt. He accepts that burden when he takes a 21-year oath of abstinence, and he prospers in his freedom.

When his wife returns, he seeks to make amends to her for the wrong she suffered at his hands. He is genuinely contrite, but he remains impulsive. He is impetuous in giving affection to Farfrae and then in feeling anger toward the younger man. He insists on rejecting Elizabeth-Jane when he discovers that she is not his daughter.

He does not learn the importance of love until he has lost both his prosperity and his position in the town. When he is completely in despair, he discovers that he cannot take the revenge on Farfrae that he had planned. He also discovers that Elizabeth-Jane's affection for him is "a pin-point of light" in the darkness.

Henchard's suffering is the result of his own actions, and he acts as he does because of his rash and impetuous nature. When he accepts Elizabeth-Jane's love, he is a changed man, but he has rashly lied to her real father about her death. He leaves Casterbridge and finally dies alone, tended only by one of his former workmen, because of that rash lie. Henchard accepts the results of his actions: his character determines his fate.

## Question 6.
What makes Elizabeth-Jane's role in the novel special?

**Answer**
Elizabeth-Jane can be shown to play a role in the novel differing from that of any of the other characters. All other characters in *The Mayor of Casterbridge* can be divided into one

of two groups: the old and the new. Susan, the furmity woman, the weather prophet, the townspeople, and especially Henchard are all part of the old rural way of life. Lucetta, Farfrae, Newson are the inhabitants of a new world with a new way of life. All the characters, except Elizabeth-Jane, are aligned either with the new or the old. Elizabeth-Jane stands between the two groups. It is no accident that she is sometimes Henchard's daughter, sometimes Newson's daughter. She is a modern woman in her craving for education, and yet from a moral standpoint, she belongs to the past. When we see her in discussion with Lucetta, we are keenly aware of Elizabeth-Jane's link with what is best in the past.

Elizabeth-Jane's position is clarified in a central scene of the novel. Farfrae has brought a piece of farm machinery to the market place beneath Lucetta's windows. Before going down to the market, Lucetta must decide which of two dresses to keep. After long meditation, which helps the reader to the realization that more is at stake here than just a dress, Lucetta chooses the red dress and says that she will be "the cherry colored person." When she and Elizabeth-Jane descend to the market place, all of the principals of the novel are present. A new agricultural machine is on display. This machine, more than anything else in the novel, is the symbol of the passing of rural England. Farfrae is responsible for the machine's presence in town; Henchard ridicules the machine. Lucetta's alliance with the machine is immediate and, as befits a character completely physical, is not an intellectual alliance. "Among all the agriculturists gathered round, the only appropriate possessor of the new machine seemed to be Lucetta, because she alone rivalled it in color."

Elizabeth-Jane, seeing value in both the old and the new, accepts the machine but laments the loss of the hand sower: "Then the romance of the sower is gone for good." Elizabeth-Jane's great strength is that she realizes the old must adapt itself to the new if it is to survive at all. She is a master at such adaptation and in the end is the only character who is able to respond to both Farfrae and Henchard. She shows that the old need not necessarily be destroyed in the wake of the new. In the end, Elizabeth-Jane is able to act as intermediary between the past and the future. The rural way of life can adapt those aspects of industrialization that are amenable to its continued existence, and at the same time retain those elements of the past that preserve the emotional and social richness of traditional cultural patterns.

# Question 7.
What part does love play in *The Mayor of Casterbridge*?

# Answer
Much of this novel is devoted to Henchard's tragic search for affection and his ultimate realization that "What he sacrificed in sentiment was worth as much as he had gained in substance." Henchard's business ventures prove disastrous and, at the same time, so do his attempts to establish warm and loving relationships. Henchard makes his first attempt at a fulfilling relationship with Farfrae, and fails. Henchard befriends the younger man but becomes increasingly bitter about Farfrae's growing successes. Henchard's initial feeling of warm affection is precisely the complicating factor. On two occasions, Henchard has Farfrae in his power, and twice he is unable to harm the Scotsman. Henchard can never completely obliterate the affection he has for Farfrae and is, consequently, in a state of raging frustration. He is unable to love or hate completely.

Henchard's interlude with Lucetta is empty and shallow, and he becomes aware of her only when she is on the verge of marriage with Farfrae. Henchard confuses jealousy with love, and his depression over Lucetta's rejection of him is not because of love, but of enraged pride.

Henchard does not love Susan, but he is thoughtful enough to try to make her happy and content. When Susan dies, Henchard turns to Elizabeth-Jane, only to find that she is actually Newson's daughter. Elizabeth-Jane returns his love and seems to make even the humiliation of working for his former employee bearable to Henchard. Newson's return to Casterbridge threatens this new-found happiness, which means so much to Henchard that for the first time in his life he tells a clear and unmistakable lie. He tells Newson that Elizabeth-Jane is dead, managing with this act to destroy his own happiness. Elizabeth-Jane turns from Henchard and leaves him an empty and tragic shell of a man.

Once again, Henchard has confused love with possession. When he returns to Casterbridge to give Elizabeth-Jane the goldfinch, Henchard has recognized the tragic flaw in his character and for the first time manages to behave in a selfless manner. He plans to keep out of "Casterbridge street till evening, lest he should mortify Farfrae and his bride." His thoughts are not of himself and his own possible embarrassment — contrast this with Henchard's earlier fear of discovery during his visit to the weather prophet — but only of Elizabeth-Jane's happiness. "He only hoped that Elizabeth-Jane had obtained a better home than had been hers at a former time." In the Farfraes' home, he catches a glimpse of Elizabeth-Jane that "made his heart ache." He sees Newson in the role of Elizabeth-Jane's father and becomes greatly agitated. "He was no longer the man to stand these reverses unmoved." Unfortunately, the character of a lifetime cannot be completely changed simply because its possessor recognizes the tragedy to which it has led. Henchard speaks with Elizabeth-Jane with "proud superiority." "Before she could collect her thoughts, Henchard went out from her rooms . . . and she saw him no more." He is too demoralized to defend himself by explaining why he lied to Newson.

When Henchard's gift bird is found dead in its cage, Elizabeth-Jane, "buried the starved little singer, and from that hour her heart softened toward the self-alienated man."

Henchard does not live to learn either how loving the feelings are that Elizabeth-Jane has for him, or how acute her insights are into his character. The death of the bird foreshadows Henchard's death; for the bird is Henchard, save that Henchard is in a cage of his own making, starving not for want of food but for want of love. However, his token of repentance was sincere and, finally, successful. The novel ends with Elizabeth-Jane's love for her stepfather.

## Question 8.
What is the significance of music in *The Mayor of Casterbridge*?

## Answer
Music is important as a means of expressing emotion. Farfrae impresses the townspeople at the Three Mariners with his emotional songs about Scotland. Henchard also responds to this singing. When he challenges Farfrae to fight with the intention of killing the younger man, he is moved and unable to take the final step of his revenge when he hears Farfrae humming "Auld Lang Syne," a song that Farfrae had sung on his first night in Casterbridge.

At the lowest point of his despair, Henchard wishes that he could sing. He longs for music, as a soothing influence and as a means of expressing the emotions he feels. When Henchard is first seen in the novel, he is reading a ballad. His love of music is constant throughout his life, and indicates an emotional depth that remains almost completely hidden.

## Question 9.
How do Lucetta and Elizabeth-Jane serve to make each other's character clearer?

## Answer
Lucetta is a sophisticated woman of the world who artfully displays herself to best advantage. Elizabeth-Jane is an unsophisticated girl who behaves artlessly. Lucetta changes her name, from Le Sueur to Templeman, to mask the past. Elizabeth-Jane changes hers, from Newson to Henchard, to please the man she thinks is her father and to accept the past. Elizabeth-Jane is honest, modest and concerned with propriety. Thus, she questions the "respectability" of the furmity tent. Lucetta has no such concern for propriety, as her indiscreet behavior with Henchard shows.

The behavior of the two women in their relationships with Farfrae underlines the differences in their characters. Lucetta arranges herself on the sofa and flirts; Elizabeth-Jane does not reveal her true feelings for Farfrae because she is shy and, later, because Henchard has forbidden their continued relationship. Both women are unusually sensitive to other people's feelings. Lucetta uses her insight for her own selfish ends; Elizabeth-Jane uses it to relieve suffering. We see this in Lucetta's skilful handling of Farfrae to further her own happiness and in Elizabeth-Jane's handling of Henchard to further his happiness.

When the two women meet, Elizabeth-Jane looks to Lucetta for advice and assistance. Before long, however, the women exchange roles, and Lucetta comes to Elizabeth-Jane for advice. Lucetta tells Elizabeth-Jane about her past and asks the younger woman's advice on a course of future action. Elizabeth-Jane tells Lucetta that she must keep her oath to Henchard, but Lucetta ignores the advice. She is too self-centered and vain to send Henchard away, and too unscrupulous to reveal her past to Farfrae.

The contrasts between the two women are clear. They are opposites in almost every respect. Lucetta's behavior makes Elizabeth-Jane's attention to propriety seem naïve, but Elizabeth-Jane's honesty and sincerity expose the evil of Lucetta's artfulness and deception.

Both women have strength, and Hardy describes the contrast between them to emphasize the differences between two kinds of strength.

## Question 10.
Discuss *The Mayor of Casterbridge* as a tragedy.

### Answer
The style of the novel suggests classical tragedy. First, the plot of *The Mayor of Casterbridge* has both the simplicity and symmetry of classical tragedy, with the steady decline of the main character's fortunes. The mythic quality of the opening scenes when Henchard sells his wife identifies the rash act that will threaten his success.

Many aspects of the classical tragedy are used in the novel: the constant reappearance of characters; the use of settings with classical architecture and associations; the townspeople who function as a chorus; the stress on folklore seen both in the use of the furmity woman and the weather prophet. Actors in classical drama wear masks; the actors in Hardy's drama wear the masks of deception and duplicity.

The rise and fall of a man of stature is the pattern of tragedy. Within that basic pattern, there is a suggestion of hope. Henchard rises to the position of mayor and falls to become a wandering laborer, but he learns and grows through the experience of failure. He learns the importance of affection and the need to accept and acknowledge the past. He learns to reach beyond pride when he returns to Casterbridge to ask Elizabeth-Jane's forgiveness. He defies the world in his will but, at the same time, acts to protect Elizabeth-Jane from suffering.

Henchard is a tragic hero in the pattern of events in his life, in his stature and in his reaction to his fate.

## Question 11.
Explain the role of pride in Henchard's fate.

### Answer
Henchard is unable to repair the damage he has done to Susan by selling her when, the next morning, he tries to find her. Although he resolves to accept the shame of what he has done, he does not want to reveal his name or identify himself to strangers

as the man who sold his wife. Thus, pride prevents him from finding Susan and Elizabeth-Jane.

When he is reunited with his family, Henchard, again hampered by pride, doesn't tell Elizabeth-Jane about the past. After Susan's death, he tells Elizabeth-Jane that she is his own daughter, only to discover Susan's note explaining that Elizabeth-Jane is Newson's daughter. Instead of confessing what has happened, Henchard keeps the secret of the past because of pride and cuts himself off from the happiness offered by Elizabeth-Jane's affection.

Pride is responsible for the destruction of Henchard's friendship with Farfrae. Henchard is angry when Farfrae crosses him in front of the other men and accuses him of tyranny with Abel Whittle. Instead of explaining why he is punishing Whittle, Henchard is hurt and angry. He feels that Farfrae is taking over his place. The fiasco of the entertainment that Henchard plans, while Farfrae's is a great success, is a blow to Henchard's pride. In his anger, he dismisses Farfrae. The next day he regrets his hasty words, but cannot humble himself to take them back and ask Farfrae's pardon.

Henchard finally wins strength to overcome his pride. He is changed by the loneliness to which he has been condemned by his pride. He responds to Elizabeth-Jane's kindness and they live together happily. Their life together is shadowed by Henchard's fear of confessing to Elizabeth-Jane his true relationship to her and the lie he told to her real father, Newson. Henchard does not tell Elizabeth-Jane these things because he is afraid that she would no longer love him if she knew. He is no longer dominated by pride but he is influenced by fear.

When Henchard leaves Casterbridge, he wants to escape the anger that Elizabeth-Jane will feel when she discovers his lie. He decides to return to ask her forgiveness because he values her affection above everything else, including his pride. In fact, he has so completely lost his pride that he cannot explain or defend his action when he meets Elizabeth-Jane.

Henchard dies alone, leaving a will in which he renounces all the ceremonies associated with death. The bitterness of his solitude is modified by the evidence of his concern for Elizabeth-Jane. He asks that she not be told of his death. He wants to save her the grief of mourning.

Although Henchard's life is dominated by pride until he recognizes the value of Elizabeth-Jane's affection, he triumphs over pride at the end of his life.

## Question 12.
To what extent is Lucetta responsible for her fate?

## Answer
Lucetta is a shallow and indiscreet character. She was thoughtless in her behavior while nursing Henchard during his illness in Jersey. She used the scandal that was the result of her behavior to press Henchard to marry her, but when she inherited money of her own, she felt free to fall in love with Farfrae. She was willing to use the past to secure a husband or to forget that past to win a different husband.

Lucetta is opportunistic, but her thoughtlessness in writing letters to Henchard and in openly snubbing her former lover makes her a victim of other opportunists. The townspeople plan the skimmity ride to shame her and to reveal her hidden past. In fact, Lucetta dies because of that revelation. She is destroyed by the past she refused to accept or confess. Her pride, as she ignores Henchard and dismisses Jopp, leads to her downfall.

## Question 13.
Discuss the significance of weather in *The Mayor of Casterbridge*.

## Answer
Hardy uses weather to comment on the action of the novel and to propel the action.

The grey, rainy November weather on the day of Henchard's marriage to Susan is appropriate to the subdued mood of the event. It also suggests that the reunion will not bring great joy to either of the partners.

The rain that falls on the day of national celebration when Henchard has spent a lot of money on an entertainment dooms his efforts to failure. His choice of the open green as the location for the festivities makes him a victim of the bad weather. Farfrae's creation of a canopy to protect his guests from the rain insures the success of his entertainment. Henchard is so angry at the contrast that he dismisses Farfrae.

Later, when Farfrae has set up a grain business in Casterbridge, Henchard resolves to prove his own superiority in business. He secretly visits a weather prophet, Mr. Fall, to find out about the weather for the harvest. On the basis of the information he gets, he buys all the grain he can. To meet his obligations, however, he is forced to sell his grain at a loss, when the weather looks like it will be fine for harvest. Farfrae buys the grain cheaply as the prospect of good harvest weather drives prices down.

However, the weather turns bad after a few days of harvesting, the price of grain rises, and Farfrae makes a handsome profit. Henchard finally goes bankrupt. The irony is that, if he had held onto his grain, he, too, would have been able to profit from the rainy harvest weather.

Hardy uses the weather conditions to influence the progress of the plot as well as to suggest the implications of specific events.

## Question 14.
In what ways may this novel be said to present the fate of rural England in a period of transition?

## Answer
Casterbridge is described as an ancient town, the center of the local agricultural district. Hardy emphasizes how little the town and its surroundings have changed over the years.

However, there are changes. The Weydon-Priors fair is busy and prosperous when Michael Henchard arrives at the beginning of the novel. Nearly 20 years later, when Susan returns with Elizabeth-Jane, the old fair is almost deserted. The furmity woman who had a tent and many customers now works in the open and is almost ignored. Five years later, she is brought into court in Casterbridge for disorderly behavior. Her source of income is gone with the changing times.

Farfrae's introduction of new machinery for sowing grain is a sign of the industrialism that will change rural life. Henchard is scornful of the machine, but his success is over. The traditional methods of doing business by word of mouth are being replaced by the careful bookkeeping that Farfrae uses.

The townspeople's revival of the skimmity ride is an attempt to renew the old traditions, but the unexpected death of Lucetta is a shock that destroys the attempt. Solomon Longways and others keep Farfrae away on the night of the skimmity ride. Their personal sympathy for Farfrae contributes to the rejection of the old traditions.

# Bibliography

Baker, Ernest A. *The History of the English Novel*, Vol. 9. New York: Barnes & Noble, Inc. (1963).

Beach, Joseph Warren. *The Technique of Thomas Hardy*. New York: Russell & Russell (1962).

Brown, Douglas. *Thomas Hardy*. London: Longmans, Green (1954).

Cecil, Lord David. *Hardy the Novelist*. London: Constable & Co., Ltd. (1943).

Daiches, David. *A Critical History of English Literature*, Vol. 2. New York: Ronald Press (1960).

Guerard, Albert J. *Thomas Hardy: The Novels and Stories*. Cambridge, Mass.: Harvard University Press (1949).

————, ed. *Hardy, A Collection of Critical Essays*. Englewood Cliffs, N.J.: Prentice-Hall, Inc. Twentieth Century Views Series (1963).

Hardy, Florence Emily. *The Early Life of Thomas Hardy, 1840-91*. New York: Macmillan & Co. (1928).

————. *The Later Years of Thomas Hardy, 1892-1928*. New York: Macmillan & Co. (1930).

Karl, Frederick R. "*The Mayor of Casterbridge*: A New Fiction Defined," *Modern Fiction Studies*, 6 (Autumn, 1961).

Millgate, Michael. *Thomas Hardy: His Career as Novelist*. London & Toronto: The Bodley Head (1971).

Smith, Anne, ed. *The Novels of Thomas Hardy*. New York: Barnes & Noble (1979).

Stewart, J.I.M. *Thomas Hardy: A Critical Biography*. London: Longmans (1971).

Vigar, Penelope. *The Novels of Thomas Hardy: Illusion and Reality*. London: The Athlone Press (1974).